Date Due

THE ANCIENT WORLD

LECTURES ON THE HISTORY OF ROMAN RELIGION

LECTURES ON THE HISTORY OF ROMAN RELIGION

FROM NUMA TO AUGUSTUS

BY

WILLIAM REGINALD HALLIDAY
B.A., B.Litt.

Rathbone Professor of Ancient History in the
University of Liverpool

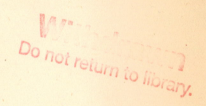
LIVERPOOL
THE UNIVERSITY PRESS OF LIVERPOOL LTD.
LONDON
HODDER AND STOUGHTON LTD.
MCMXXII
Agents for the United States
BARNES & NOBLE, INC.
105 5TH AVE., NEW YORK 3, N.Y.

Made and Printed in Great Britain
C. Tinling & Co., Ltd., 53, Victoria Street, Liverpool, and at London and Prescot

TO
WILLIAM WARDE FOWLER

αἱ δὲ τεαὶ ζώουσιν ἀηδόνες, ἧσιν ὁ πάντων
ἁρπακτὴς Ἀΐδης οὐκ ἐπὶ χεῖρα βαλεῖ.

PREFACE.

This little book does not aim at making any original contribution to knowledge. It has been written out from the notes of a course of lectures, which were actually delivered as public lectures in our Institute of Archaeology, but were primarily designed for students in the first or second year of study in the Honours School of Classics in Liverpool University. Their aim was to summarise very briefly the character and the historical development of Roman religion up to the death of Augustus. It had been intended that the story should be completed by a similar course upon the conflict of religions under the Roman Empire to be given by my friend and colleague, Mr. H. A. Ormerod. Unforeseen contingencies have caused what I hope may be only a postponement. These circumstances may be allowed to explain the meagre treatment here allotted to the introduction of Oriental cults and to the antecedents of Emperor worship, for these topics belong essentially to this second chapter in the history of Rome.

I have very strictly limited my references both

to original authorities and to specialist works. So short a survey cannot aim at more than being an introduction to larger works of a general character in which the further references will be found. I have borrowed freely from all the books mentioned below, and most extensively from Warde Fowler's *Religious Experience of the Roman People*, a book which it is as delightful as it is profitable to read again and again.

It is impossible in the effort to be concise to avoid occasional overstatement and sometimes I may have represented as fact what is disputable hypothesis. I have tried, however, to be orthodox rather than original, and I hope that in the main these lectures represent sound doctrine.

Two excellent small books upon Roman religion exist in English, though one if not both are out of print. The late Mr. J. B. Carter's *Religion of Numa and other Essays* covers much the same ground as these lectures ; Mr. Cyril Bailey's, *The Religion of Ancient Rome* deals with the religion of Numa.   In addition to the relevant articles in Dictionaries and Encyclopedias mention may also be made of the introduction to Mr. Bailey's recent edition of the Third Book of the *Fasti* of Ovid. Carter's, *The Religious Life of Ancient Rome : a study in the development of religious consciousness from the foundation of the city until the death of Gregory the Great* will be found to provide interesting reading, though the subject of these lectures forms only a small and relatively unimportant part in his design.

The two great names in this field of study are those of Wissowa and Warde Fowler. Wissowa, *Religion und Kultus der Römer* is published as a volume of Iwan Müller's, *Handbuch der Klassischen Altertumswissenschaft. Die Religion der Römer* by his pupil Aust is probably the best complete history of Roman religion upon a slightly smaller scale. Everything that Warde Fowler has written is distinguished by ripe scholarship, sound judgment and graceful presentation. Besides the great work already mentioned his *Festivals of the Roman Republic* surveys in detail the religious events of the Roman year. With *Roman Ideas of Deity in the last century of the Republic* should be read the same author's *Social Life at Rome in the Age of Cicero.* The series of papers collected in *Roman Essays and Interpretations* contain some of great importance for our subject. In particular may be mentioned " The Latin History of the word *Religio,*" " The origin of the Lar Familiaris " and " The *Carmen Saeculare* of Horace and its First Performance."

The best general account of Roman divination remains that contained in the fourth volume of Bouché Leclerq, *Histoire de la Divination dans l'Antiquité* (Paris, 1882). Upon all constitutional questions affecting religion a clear, concise, and learned summary of the facts may be found in Greenidge, *Roman Public Life.*

If an excuse be needed for adding this summary of the subject to the company of larger and better works it may perhaps be found in the fact that, if classical scholarship is temporarily under a cloud, there is nevertheless an increasing number of persons, unskilled or little skilled in the classical languages, who are interested in Greek and Roman civilisation. There are also many who are interested in comparative religion but lack a knowledge of the facts. Particularly in Roman religion these are liable to be led astray by mistaken deductions from poetical mythology. The very modesty of my scope may perhaps tempt some of them to make the acquaintance of the main facts as they are now known and possibly to pursue farther some of the problems which they raise.

W. R. HALLIDAY.

THE UNIVERSITY, LIVERPOOL,
June, 1922.

CONTENTS

LECTURE I

ONE of the main difficulties in presenting a picture of Greek religion lies in the multiplicity of the Greek states varying in their degree of civilisation. This particular difficulty does not confront the student of Roman religion. His attention is fixed upon a single stage, the seven hills which guard the ford of the Tiber, and he is concerned with the religious beliefs and practices of a single people, a group of peasant farmers whom circumstance and the force of their own character caused to become the conquerors first of Italy and in the end of the civilised world.

The subject, however, has difficulties of its own. All roads lead to Rome, and alike upon Roman character and upon Roman religion foreign influences were increasingly at work. First Greece conquered her conqueror, and then Oriental cults and modes of thought invaded the capital of the world in overwhelming force. " The Orontes " said Iuvenal in the first century of our era " has long been flowing into the Tiber."

Change of circumstance has its reaction upon character and it is a law of evolution that adaptation to change is necessary for survival. In itself the history of the development of these peasant farmers of Central Italy into the rulers of the world provides an interesting and dramatic spectacle. Hardly less interesting are the changes in national character and belief, which accompanied and were caused by these secular changes, and in fact it will be found, as indeed was to have been expected, that the stages in the history of the development of Roman religion closely correspond with the phases of the political history of Rome. The earliest stratum of religious belief and practice contains reminiscences of the prehistoric conditions of life when the pioneers settled in the forests of the Central Appenines and when civilisation and ordered life were limited to the clearings which surrounded their homesteads, and beyond which lay the forest, unknown and menacing, the domain of Silvanus, the wild spirit of the woods. Then in our earliest complete outline of Roman public worship we see the peasant households organised into a military state, the Rome whose duty it was to defend the Latin plain from the Etruscan powers and the marauding tribes of hillmen. The religion of Numa, as

the Romans called it attributing the foundation
of their religious institutions to a traditional
law-giver and king, represents the adaptation of
the religion of the farm and the household to the
needs of an organised community, a community,
however, which was still homogeneous in character and the economic and social basis of which
was purely agricultural.

The Etruscan rulers of the later monarchy
brought with them the more elaborate ceremonial of temple worship. They too laid the
foundations of Rome's secular greatness. New
interests and occupations entered the community ;
politically Rome became the acknowledged head
of the Latin League, economically commerce
began to compete with agriculture. With both
developments came new religious needs uncatered
for by the agricultural religion of Numa ; these
were met by the adoption of foreign deities,
foreign rites and foreign ways of religious thought.
The predominating influence was Greek trans-
mitted in the first place at second hand through
Etruscan or Italian channels, but as the Roman
Republic became increasingly dominant in the
Italian Peninsula direct contact with the Greek
towns of Italy accentuated the action of Greek
civilisation upon Roman. The conquest of

Tarentum in 272 B.C. led directly to the birth of
Latin literature through the agency of a Greek
captive, Livius Andronicus. It led also to the
wars with Carthage and so to the emergence of
Rome at their victorious close as a world power,
no longer a city state of peasant proprietors but
the capitalist ruler of an empire. If the political
institutions of the city state proved inadequate
to the new burden, it is not surprising that a
religious system devised to meet the needs of a
community of farmers had ceased to have much
reality for the masters of the world. The additions
which had been made to it were of the nature of
foreign accretions not the products of organic
growth.   In temper and character they were in
fact inconsistent with the system which they were
designed to supplement and the foreign elements
had swamped the native. The old Roman *numina*
had become identified with the anthropomorphic
gods of Greece and Greek mythology had been
transplanted bodily to Italy. During the desperate
strain of the war with Hannibal foreign worships
had been admitted in increasing numbers by the
state's desire to invoke supernatural aid, and their
introduction had been welcomed by the anxiety
of individuals. The emotional cults of the East
first gained a legal footing in Rome with the

introduction of the Great Mother, the nature goddess of Asia Minor, in 205 B.C.

The last hundred years of the Republic represent a century of chaos ; the religion of the city state, like its political institutions and morals had completely broken down. Scepticism and superstition tempered by philosophy not unfairly describes the religion of the upper classes and the ordinances of the established religion of the state were little more than instruments at the disposal of the political wire-puller.

Then from chaos emerged the empire and its great founder Augustus by restoring the old forms of religious observance hoped to recapture the ancient Roman character, discipline and morals upon which he perceived that Rome's great past had been securely built. He was unable however to breathe life into a system which had long been dead and imperial Rome in fact became the focus of a conflict of religions, mainly Oriental in origin, from which Christianity eventually emerged triumphant.

It will be clear from this summary of our subject that in studying the earlier stages of Roman religion the evidence of Latin literature must be handled with caution. In fact it will be advisable to put out of our minds all the stories

B

about the Roman gods which we have learned from Virgil and Ovid and the other poets. Ultimately these are Greek not Roman in origin and are likely to mislead us into drawing conclusions from some later accretion of Graeco-Roman mythology which is Roman only in appearance.

In fact it must be admitted that the religion of Numa has little direct connection with Latin literature.   Nevertheless its study may prove to be not without value even for those whose interest is primarily in the understanding of Latin literature or Roman history.   For Latin literature though derivative is not merely an imitation and through a borrowed medium it yet expresses an independent national character.   In the long run, whether in individuals or in societies, character is the mainspring and apart from its intrinsic interest, the study of the religious beliefs and practices of the early Romans reveals something of the hard rock of disciplined character upon which the fortunes of that great imperial race were ultimately based.

The word religion is itself the bequest of Latin to the languages of modern Europe and its history is instructive.[1] *Religio* means primarily " the

---

[1] See Warde Fowler, *Roman Essays and Interpretations*, pp. 7-15.

natural fear or awe which semi-civilised man feels in the presence of what he cannot explain." From this developed the secondary meaning of religious duties, the obligation to perform which is prompted by *religio* in its earlier sense. Later it came to mean first the whole sphere of worship as viewed from the standpoint of the philosopher and finally a particular and individual competing division of that sphere of worship. In these last two senses the word is used to-day as when we speak of " Varieties of Religious Experience " or contrast the religion of Christianity with that of Islam : it is the first two meanings of the word however which concern the student of the religion of Numa.

Religio then is the feeling of awe with which the unknown inspired the early settler in Central Italy. He recognised that there were forces actually or potentially at work in natural processes and in remarkable natural objects or phenomena. He appreciated the mysteries of birth and growth, of the annual ripening of the corn, or of the fortunate increase of his herds, at least so far as to realise that factors not within his control contributed to these essential happenings. In the thunderbolt or in the lightning a strange and unintelligible power was manifested and as he looked beyond the limits of his clearing at the forest, he felt the presence in its dark recesses of forces which he did not know but feared. This feeling has been recaptured as a sentiment by the most sophisticated of Latin courtiers in describing the sacred grove upon the Aventine.

> "lucus Aventino suberat niger ilicis umbra,
>   quo posses viso dicere ' numen inest.' "

A glance at that dark mysterious grove would bring to your lips the words : " There is a *numen* in it."

Numen is a word for which no English equivalent exists. It is etymologically connected with the verb *nuere* and connotes the idea of will power. It seems to mean that incalculable force the intervention of which in any process or action makes the difference between success or failure, safety or disaster. It is this force which arouses the feeling of awe, *religio* in its primary sense, and it is the object of *religio*, in its secondary sense of the performance of religious duties, to harness it, as it were, in the service of man or to prevent its adverse operation. *Numen* however is not a universal concept of a single force immanent throughout the natural world. Every object of awe and every functional action has its particular *numen* upon which the safety or success of the worshipper depends. But at the same time, *numina* are not gods. They have no personality; they are not conceived as possessing human shape; their sex is indeterminate. Indeed it is only in action that *numina* manifest themselves and it was only with their manifestation that the early Roman was interested. Practical and unimaginative, he remained otherwise quite incurious, indulged in no speculation as to their nature or origin and invented no stories about them. Early Roman religion is consequently devoid both of mythology and of images. It has nothing of the aesthetic appeal of Greek anthropomorphism. And if it gives little scope to the artistic imagination, it leaves little room for moral fervour. The early Roman, in Cicero's words, did not ask the gods to make him good but to give him health and wealth. His religion provides no opportunity for the development of a personal emotional relation between worshipper and the object of worship as do religious systems in which gods are conceived upon the analogy of human personality.

In fact, the Romans from the very beginning were an unimaginative people; to compensate however they were shrewd, hard-headed and practical, by instinct a race of lawyers rather than a race of poets or philosophers. There is indeed a legal almost a contractual air about their whole religion. The purpose of acts of worship was to secure the aid of the appropriate *numen* or *numina* in the matter then in hand. It was assumed that provided the proper rites were performed in the right manner at the right time and in the right place there was almost an obligation upon the power concerned to exercise a favourable activity. If on the other hand there was the least flaw in the procedure, however unintentional, the whole process was invalid. From the outset there was therefore a strong tendency to formalism and a disposition to entrust the performance of the necessary rites to the expert who knew how they should properly be performed.

Another characteristically Roman feature is the complete lack of individualism in early Roman religion. Its true subdivisions are the religious observances of the household, of the farm and of the state and throughout it is primarily the welfare of the appropriate group not that of an individual which is the object of religious ceremonies. Even in the face of death no hope or fear of personal immortality confronted the early Roman. The family it is true was immortal but the individual passed at death to join an unindividualised group of ancestral departed spirits, the *di parentum* or, as they were more usually known in later days, *di manes*.

The force of this intense group solidarity, of which the group voting of all Roman political assemblies is a different manifestation, is a little difficult for the modern mind to appreciate. But no doubt in this complete subordination of the individual is to be seen the same temper of mind which inspired the patriotism of the early Roman and provided those many heroic examples which Livy delighted to hold up before a more degenerate age. Undoubtedly it was the feeling that the interests of Rome came before those of any individual Roman that was one of the most powerful factors in Rome's greatness.

It is easy too to underrate the value of an exact and regular performance of ritual acts. The daily worship in the family and the regularly recurrent ceremonies of the farm or of the state, had in their mere performance a disciplinary value, while participation in them emphasised unconsciously the solidarity of the group and the common interests and mutual duties of its individual members.

LECTURE II

THE unit of early Roman society is the family, of which the *pater familias* is the natural representative. Upon him the other members depend; they are " in his hand," to use the Roman legal phrase, and completely subject to his authority. He is the sole trustee and administrator of family property and, in return, it is his duty to support and defend it. But true to the instinct of group solidarity, which has already been noticed, the early Roman state may be said to consist of an aggregate of families rather than an aggregate of individuals. It is the household, not the individual, which supplies the lowest common multiple of society, and the *familia* includes not only father, mother, sons and daughters, but slaves and servants as well.

The primitive household in pre-Roman days lived in a round wigwam with a central hearth placed beneath a hole in the apex of the conical roof by which the smoke escaped. Models of such houses, which were used as funerary urns, have

24

been found in the Iron Age cemetery upon the site of the Roman Forum, and their form survived in the circular temple of Vesta. Although in very early days the oblong house, which was borrowed perhaps from Greek or Etruscan models, took the place of this primitive circular dwelling, for long it consisted of but a single room with a roof sloping inwards to a central vent above the hearth.

With the family and the structure, in which it lived, the objects of family worship were connected—Ianus, the Genius, the Lar of the Family, Vesta and the Penates. These represent, as it were, functions of the family existence and none of them were originally invested with any corporeal form or thought of as individual personalities.

Ianus represents the *numen* of the door and no doubt owes his importance to the insecurity of the early settler's life. The door is the breach in the defences of the homestead through which evil whether spiritual or material can most easily enter. This very natural feeling, which has left its mark upon the religious and superstitious practices of peoples in all parts of the world, may be illustrated by Roman burial custom. When the dead were carried out for burial the corpse was always carried feet first through the door for fear that the ghost should find his way back through it.

Similarly, if a person was falsely reported dead, upon his return home he might not enter through the door but was made to descend through a hole made for the purpose in the roof. Analogous fears, as will be seen, attached for similar reasons to city gates. Of the family cult of Ianus the details are unfortunately lacking. It is legitimate to suppose that its performance will have been peculiarly the business of the *pater familias* the natural defender of the homestead.

The Genius represents the life of the family. The word is etymologically connected with *gignere* " to beget," and the idea implicit is that of the procreative force which makes it possible for the family to exist or continue. Thus the marriage bed was called the *lectus genialis*. Every man is a potential father of a family and hence has a Genius, every woman is a potential mother and has a corresponding *numen* a Iuno. In the course of time the Genius came to be thought of as the spiritual double of an individual man, and this idea was even extended later to cities as, for instance, Genius Romae, the spiritual essence or luck of Rome. The fundamental notion however seems to have been less individual. " The individual " said the biologist Weissman " is an incident in the life of the germ plasm." Somewhat similarly the Genius was originally regarded as the *numen* of the life of the family which continues through the incidents of its successive generations. This force was manifest in the head of the household, the father of the family for the time being in any given generation. Upon his birthday the whole household including slaves and freedmen joined in worship of the Genius Domus, the genius of the household. No doubt this very natural association of the life of the family with the life of the head of the household helped to promote the individualisation of the Genius. The later view, which regarded it as the spiritual double of an individual man, was also influenced by the Greek belief in a δαίμων, a guardian spirit that accompanied each man from his birth.[1]

The Lares have been wrongly thought to represent the spirits of dead ancestors of the family. This view was current even among Roman antiquaries of Augustan date but it is none the less mistaken. It was derived, as were so many of the later Roman ideas about their religion, from Greek influences.

The Lares were originally the tutelary powers

---

[1] Menander (Kock), *Frag.* 550. ἅπαντι δαίμων ἀνδρὶ συμπαρίσταται, | εὐθὺς γενομένῳ, μυσταγωγὸς τοῦ βίου | ἀγαθός

of the clearing which the early farmer had reclaimed from the forest and they continued in Cicero's day to be "worshipped on the farm within sight of the house." The ancestors of the Romans were not a people of village communities but lived in isolated homesteads surrounded by the family holding. Where the family property met the boundary of the forest or that of a neighbour's land the tutelary *numina* of the property were worshipped. Thus arose the worship of the Lares Compitales, the Lares of the Crossways, *i.e.* the intersecting boundaries. In classical times at such a *compitum* there was a small shrine containing as many doors as there were properties that met. In each property was an altar set back 15 feet from the door to enable the worshipper to perform the necessary rites upon his own ground. The expression however Lares and Penates, as meaning "hearth and home," is a *cliché* which has descended to our modern speech from the patriotic rhetoric of ancient Rome and in fact one of the Lares had entered the house, not as a dead ancestor nor as a member of the family in our sense of the word but as a member of the Roman *familia* or household. For the Lar Familiaris came indoors with the farm hands and the cult remained the special charge of the *vilica* or bailiff's wife. If the Genius represents the life force of the family considered as a group of blood relations, the Lar is the " luck " of the household, the economic unit. Upon the new moon, first quarter and full moon as fixed by the calendar, *i.e.* upon the Kalends, Nones and Ides of each month, the family offered him worship. With this cult the family fortunes were intimately associated. Upon all family occasions, such as a birth, wedding, or funeral, offerings were made to the Lar Familiaris and even upon the departure or return of a member of the family from a long journey.

Naturally enough the care of the powers inside the house fell to the housewife and her daughters. These were Vesta, the *numen* of the hearth, and the Penates, the *numina* of the *penus* or store-cupboard. Although in later times images of the Penates were often set upon the table, neither Vesta nor Penates were originally conceived as possessing corporeal form and, even after Greek influence had become paramount, Vesta was never represented in family cult by any image or statue. At the mid-day meal of the early Roman family the table was spread in front of the hearth in the centre of the single room which was kitchen and living room combined. Beyond the hearth was the store-cupboard, upon the table the *salinum* or saltcellar and a sacrificial plate (*patella*) with a piece of salt cake upon it. Round the table sat the whole *familia*, the farm hands upon the lower benches (*subsellia*). At every meal the head of the household threw an offering of a piece of salted cake from the sacrificial plate into the flame of Vesta. This daily ritual of prayer and sacrifice at meal time survived in form even into the days of luxury and it remained the practice to observe a pause in the banquet while an offering was sent out to the kitchen, the meal being resumed only when the news had been brought back that the offering had been made and had been propitiously received.

It is unfortunate, though not perhaps surprising, that we possess so little detailed information about family worship. Its observance goes back beyond the beginnings of Roman history and it persisted unaltered in essentials as long as paganism lasted. Although in the period of Rome's greatness the sense of home became lost in the enormous and elaborate households of the rich, while the miserable lot of the urban poor lodged in tenements and cast after death into a common burial pit deprived these unfortunates of any real family life, there was always a middle class. At the close of paganism the Theodosian Code bears witness to the vitality of what was, perhaps, the healthiest element in Roman religion. " Let no man in any place in any city make sacrifice or worship the Lar with burnt offering, or the Genius with wine, or the Penates with perfumes—let them light no lamp, burn no incense, hang no garlands."

The observances of family cult were perhaps too much a matter of course to give rise to description in Roman literature but, meagre as is our knowledge of them, it is clear that religion entered largely into the trivial round of family life from day to day and a sober atmosphere of religious duty and a religious routine exerted their beneficial influence upon Roman character.

If religion formed a part of the daily routine of family life it will be no surprise to find that the great crises of existence, birth, marriage and death, were of religious moment. When a child was born it was placed upon the ground and ceremonially raised in his arms by the father in token of his acknowledgment of its paternity. The naming festival for boys was held upon the ninth day and for girls upon the eighth day after birth. Until a name had been given the infant was held to be in peculiar danger from hostile influences such as the *striga* or vampire witch, who flies in the shape of an owl to suck infants' blood. In this belief the Romans were by no means singular. The danger of infancy before christening is a world wide superstition. It is for example during this interval that the Irish peasant mother most dreaded the removal of her child by the Little People and the substitution of a changeling. At Rome immediately after birth special precautions were taken against hostile influences. An offering was made to Picumnus and Pilumnus, two rather obscure powers connected apparently with fertility, and at night three men armed with an axe, a stake and a broom proceeded to the threshold, which constituted, as we have already noticed, a point of danger where hostile influences might gain an entry into the house. The men with the axe and stake struck the threshold in order to drive away or frighten off Silvanus, the wild spirit of the forest, while the third man swept away with his broom any hostile powers which might be trying to get in. Characteristically the religious lawyers of Rome represented these actions as efficacious in virtue of three *numina*—Intercidona, the hacking power, Pilumnus, the power of the stake, and Deverra the sweeping power.

The day of naming the child was observed as a

family feast at which friends brought presents for the child. With the name a boy received the *bulla*, a circular case containing an amulet, which with the *toga praetexta*, a garment with a purple stripe, was worn until the age of seventeen, when the boy became a man and put on the *toga virilis*. The purple stripe upon the toga was originally intended to serve the same purpose as the *bulla i.e.* to avert the Evil Eye and other influences peculiarly dangerous to children. This prophylactic virtue of the purple stripe is the reason why the *toga praetexta* at Rome was the distinctive dress alike of childhood and of the highest priestly and secular magistracies.

The change from childhood to manhood signified by the change of dress took place usually upon March 17th during the earlier Republic (under the late Republic and Empire, when enrolment in the citizen army was no longer a matter of moment to the state, the date for assuming the responsibilities of manhood varied) and was accompanied by sacrifice and a visit to the Capitolian temple.

Marriage similarly, was sanctified by religion. In its older patrician form, *confarreatio* (the eating together of the sacred spelt), it was definitely a religious ceremony and might almost be called a sacrament. The bride and bridegroom sat upon

c

two chairs placed together and covered with a lambskin and after making bloodless offerings to Iupiter they ate together a cake made of the sacred spelt. But even in the later form of civil marriage, *coemptio*, the essential act of joining the hands was solemnised with sacrifice.

The ceremony of bringing the bride to the husband's house was performed with a number of rites, which find their parallels in European folklore. She was forcibly abducted by the bridegroom's friends amid lamentations of her own, nuts were scattered and ribald songs were sung and upon reaching her new home she was lifted over the threshold. Amongst the numerous minor ceremonies of marriage, most of which are common to many peoples, one characteristically Roman rite is perhaps worth noticing. The girl at marriage left one family for another; she passed " from the hand " of her father to that of her husband, from the Lares of her father's household to the Lares of her husband's. This fact was emphasised by a symbolical action. The bride carried three copper coins, one of these she ceremonially presented to her husband, one to the Lar Familiaris of her new home and one to the Lar Compitalis, the presiding spirit of the homestead.

Throughout their history the Romans practised

both burial and cremation. In classical times cremation was the more usual method of disposal of the corpse though burial was thought to be the older custom. It was for this reason that when the body was burned a single bone was preserved and given burial. In fact, however, although in the Bronze Age there is a distinction of burial custom corresponding to racial difference and the people of the *Terremare* burned their dead while the Italian natives practised inhumation, in the cemeteries of the early Iron Age the mixed race, which constituted the immediate ancestors of the Romans, already practised both methods of disposal.

In the funeral ceremonies of early Rome there is no trace of a worship of the dead man nor indeed of any belief in personal survival. The placing of Charon's penny in the mouth was a custom later taken over, together with the eschatology which Latin poets have made familiar, from Greek sources. In the purely Roman ceremonies of funeral the ideas which find expression are the fear common to the majority of mankind of the contagion of death, the pathos of the last farewell and the continuity of the life of the family. At the moment of death the heir bent over the dying man to catch his last breath, then the eyes of the dead man were closed, and amid lamentations, in which the dead man was called by name, the corpse was washed, anointed, dressed in the robes of the highest office, which the deceased had held during life, and laid in state in the *atrium* with the feet pointing to the door ; the bier was adorned with flowers and wreaths and watched by a slave watchman.

For a period normally varying from three to seven days the body thus lay in state. During this time the fire was extinguished in the house and a bough of pine or cypress was erected outside the door to warn passers by and particularly religious functionaries, for whom any contact with death was strictly taboo, that a corpse lay within. The funeral procession took place at night by torchlight. Accompanied by musicians and professional mourners the body was carried to the grave or pyre and laid to rest outside the city walls. The ceremony concluded with the last farewell three times uttered over the tomb :

animamque sepulchro
Condimus et magna supremum voce ciemus.

Funerals in Rome as elsewhere gave occasion for extravagant expenditure which sumptuary laws were powerless to check. Most elaborate

were the public funerals of distinguished states-
men the ceremonial of which, though perhaps of
Etruscan origin, appealed alike to the Roman
genius for stately processional ceremonial and to
the Roman sense of family continuity. The public
funeral took place by day and in the procession,
which made its way to the Forum, all the members
of the family living and dead were represented.
In the *atrium* of a noble's house were hung the
death masks (*imagines*) of his distinguished ancestors and upon the occasion of a funeral these were
worn by actors clad in the insignia of the highest
office of state to which the ancestors thus imper-
sonated had respectively attained. At the head
came the musicians followed by the male choir,
which took the place of the professional mourners
of humbler funerals. Behind these were dancers
and manumitted slaves of the deceased. Between
them and the bier drove the ancestors imper-
sonated in the way above described and attended
by the freedmen of the dead man. Upon the bier
the corpse was carried lying in state and open to
the view or if for any reason it was enclosed in a
coffin a wooden effigy clad in the official insignia
of the dead man was displayed. At the Forum a
halt was called. The ancestors descended and
seated themselves in a circle upon ivory chairs,

while the next of kin mounted the *rostrum* and delivered a laudatory speech. The procession then reformed and continued its way to the place of burial.

After a funeral the living members of the family purified themselves with fire and water and the house, in which the death had taken place, was purified by the sacrifice of a sow and the sweeping out of all refuse. For nine days the surviving relatives remained unclean and might not mix with their fellow citizens. Upon the ninth day an offering took place at the tomb which was followed by a feast at which mourning dress was put off and the guests were clad in gala attire (*albati*). This concluded the mourning. Upon anniversaries of death and burial and upon certain fixed dates the relatives visited the tomb and made offerings of salt cake, bread soaked in wine, and flowers. But these rites seem to have been commemorative in character. It was necessary for the dead man to receive due rites of burial and incumbent upon his heir to see that they were carried out, but there is no trace in early times of the worship of an individual dead man.

At death the spirit was thought to join the unindividualised Di Manes. Once more Roman notions are found to show a natural preference for collective concepts. It is true that in the Latin poets and in sepulchral inscriptions of the first century B.C. the word *Manes* is used in the sense of the spirit of an individual dead person, but this usage is nowhere found in earlier Latin nor is there any evidence that before he came under the influence of Greek ideas the Roman looked forward to personal immortality.

The collective ancestral dead, Di Manes, to whom as powers of the lower world offerings were made and who figure in the ritual of *devotio*, by which a Roman general at the cost of his own life could consecrate his opponent's army to death and defeat, were regarded in historical times as powers which were upon the whole beneficent, though it is possible that they were earlier regarded with fear. Upon certain days when the *mundus* was opened they were thought to revisit the living. This *mundus* was a circular pit closed by a stone and the dates upon which it was opened, all of which are appropriate to agricultural processes[1], lend colour to the view that it originated in a primitive subterranean storehouse in which the seed corn of the community was kept. Such

[1] The dates are August 24th, the day before the Opiconsivia, and October 5th and November 8th, which Warde Fowler suggests were the dates upon which the seed corn for the sowing of *far* and finer kinds of wheat was taken out. See *Roman Essays*, pp. 24 foll.

an association of powers of the underworld with fertility is of course quite a common phenomenon among primitive peoples.

Two festivals, or series of festivals in honour of the dead were marked in the calendar. The Parentalia in February, the month of purification, lasted from February 13—21 and were concluded upon February 22nd by the feast of Cara Cognatio or Caristia, a love feast for the survivors of the family. The motive of the festival seems rather to have been a solemn family commemoration than the placation of angry or malevolent spirits of the dead.

The Lemuria however held upon the 9th, 11th and 13th of May, at a time when the crops were at a critical stage, was definitely a festival of aversion. About the public ritual of this occasion we possess no information but Ovid has given us an account of the domestic ceremonial at the conclusion of which at midnight the father of the family walking barefoot spat out black beans without looking backwards reciting the charm : "with these I redeem me and mine." Then after clanking brazen vessels, he dismissed the spirits of the dead to their own place with the formula nine times repeated : " Depart ye Manes of my fathers."

LECTURE III

THE RELIGION OF THE FARM

" Fortunatus et ille deos qui novit agrestes."

THE religion of the farm like the religion of the
home survived the early religion of the State.
Long after the ordinances of Numa had become
obsolete in the city the rustic population of
Italy continued to observe the simple ritual of
their fathers. Charming little vignettes of these
rustic festivals are to be found in the Latin poets,
particularly in Tibullus, and Cato's practical
treatise upon agriculture has preserved for us
some interesting facts.[1] Of the ritual of the farm
it is true that we possess no complete account, but
the calendar of Numa enables us to form an idea
of the ceremonies of the farmer's year. For the
chief pre-occupation of the festivals there enumer-
ated is with the welfare of the crops and herds
and the document in fact represents the farmer's
calendar taken over by the state and systematised
to suit the needs of the larger community.

[1] Readers of Pater will remember the delightful sketch of rustic religion
in the first chapter of *Marius the Epicurean.*

A word therefore must be said as to the nature
and date of this evidence. A number of fragments
of official Roman calendars have fortunately survived. The documents themselves are of imperial
date but upon all existing examples a number of
festivals are cut in larger capitals than the
rest. There can be no reasonable doubt that
these festivals in large capitals represent the
older fixed festivals of the state preserved
apart by Roman conservatism and distinguished
from later accretions. By internal evidence this
list can be approximately dated. Quirinus figures
among the divinities mentioned and therefore the
list must have been drawn up after the incorporation of the Quirinal settlement in the Roman
state. On the other hand there is no mention
of Diana, the goddess of the Latin League, nor
of the great triad of the Capitol, Iupiter, Iuno
and Minerva. The list must therefore have been
completed before the later monarchy when Rome
under her Etruscan rulers became the head of
the Latin League and the worship of this Etruscan
triad of divinities was inaugurated. The list of
festivals may therefore be claimed to represent
with fair completeness the religion of Numa.

The creation of a calendar indeed followed
necessarily from the organisation of religion by

the state. It was essential to the welfare of the community, especially to one the religious attitude of which displayed so marked a legal bias, that its members should not offend by the omission of religious ceremonies upon the proper occasions nor by the commission of acts of secular business upon holy days. In order that the citizens should have the necessary guidance the *pontifices* declared upon the Kalends (new moon) of each month the date upon which the Nones (first quarter), would fall. Upon the Nones the *rex sacrorum* proclaimed the names and dates of the religious festivals of the month and upon what days it was lawful or unlawful to transact secular business. Originally the knowledge of the calendar, like that of all religious law, was the monoply of the aristocratic college of priests but inevitably in course of time announcement was supplemented by publication. In 304 B.C. for the first time the calendar was exhibited in the marketplace and in 189 B.C. one of the consuls adorned the temple of Hercules and the Muses with a permanent record of the dates of the regular festivals. Finally after the successful adjustment of the lunar to the solar year in 45 B.C., the reformed calendar of Iulius Cæsar was copied and set up in Rome and other towns, and thanks to the

survival of a number of complementary fragments
of these inscriptions we possess the Roman
calendar practically complete.

The first column of these calendars marks the
secular weeks from market day to market day.
The second column gives the days of the month
and against each of them in the third is set a
letter to denote the character of the day : F
(*fastus*) and N (*nefastus*) or NP indicate days upon
which secular business might or might not be
undertaken.   C (*comitialis*) indicates a day upon
which business might be transacted in the public
assemblies.   Eight days, all of which fall immediately before some festival or before the Ides
(full moon), which in every month was sacred to
Iupiter, are marked EN (*endotercisus*).   Upon
these the morning and evening were *nefastus*
but the middle of the day was free for secular
affairs.   Against March 24th and May 24th is
entered Q.R.C.F. (*quando rex comitiavit fas*).
Upon these days the king presided in the *Comitia
Curiata* for the sanctioning of wills and other
religio-legal business and secular affairs were therefore prohibited until the assembly had dispersed.
The isolated entry Q.S.T.D.F. (*quando stercus
delatum fas*) against June 15th is explained below.[1]

1 See below, p. 54.

The next column contains the older fixed festivals written in large capitals and is followed by a list of the festivals subsequently added. These and the often valuable comments upon religious matters which are found in some examples are always cut in smaller capitals.

In the calendar of Numa then we have a fairly complete record of the farmer's year which, as the numerical month names of our own calendar still testify, began in March. In addition to the festivals of the calendar may be considered some which are known from other sources but do not appear in the calendar, not because they were of more recent date but because the date of their incidence was not fixed but depended upon the forwardness of the crops in any given year.

March, the month of Mars, is the month of the spring's awakening. It opened with the "moving" of the sacred shields of Mars (*ancilia*), a ceremonial which began upon March 1st and concluded a fortnight later. Upon the first the *ancilia*, which were large oblong shields of the shape of a figure of eight like those depicted in Mycenaean art, were taken from the sacrarium Martis in the Regia and borne in procession by the *Salii* to a different fixed resting place each night until their return to the Regia upon March 24th.

A feature of this procession was the dancing
of the armed priests who were clad in the full war
paint of the early Italian warrior with tall conical
caps upon their heads. Their leaping dance,
the *tripudium* or threestep, was accompanied by
the clashing of rods or spears against the shields and
the chanting of the old Latin hymns (*axamenta*),
the meaning of which had become unintelligible
to the Roman of the Augustan age. In these
hymns there is repeated invocation of Mamurius
which is an early form of Mars. The analogy
between these Roman armed priests and the
Kouretes of Crete, who clashed their weapons
and invoked Zeus Kouros in a leaping dance,
impressed Dionysius of Halicarnassus as it has
impressed modern students of the classical
religions and although the analogy would be
more helpful if we were better informed in detail
about the Kouretes, certain facts about their
ritual are clear which help to account for the
Saliaric dance. Mythology tells how they clashed
their armour round the infant Zeus to protect
him from the attack of the Titans and the clashing
of armour or the beating of metal in order to
make a noise, which will frighten away evil
influences, is a frequent practice in primitive
religion all over the world. A late copy of the

chant which was sung by the Kouretes has been
recently discovered and this throws light upon
the leaping dance. "Leap" they sang "for full
jars, and leap for fleecy flocks and leap for fields
of fruit and for hives to bring increase." The
object then of the leaping dance of the *Salii* in
the month of spring was probably in order to
increase the fertility of the coming year. The
original idea, no doubt, was to secure by sympathetic magic that the crops should spring up
with the same vigour as the dancers. The clashing
of weapons was to drive away evil influences and
possibly at the same time to imitate thunder and
thus to secure an adequate supply of rain during
the year. The double motive is by no means
incredible and examples of the amalgamation of
two really different motives in a single ritual are
more frequent than is always supposed.

Of the Liberalia on March 17th but little is
known. In later times Liber was identified by the
Romans with the Greek god Dionysos but the
original Latin deity had probably nothing to do
with wine. Liber and Libera seem in fact to
have represented male and female aspects of
fertility. Upon this day during the early Republic
the boys who had reached the age of seventeen
put off the garb of childhood, donned the *toga*

virilis and were registered as recruits in the citizen army.

April, " the month of opening " was of some importance in the farmer's year. Upon April 15th took place the Fordicidia, a festival in honour of Mother Earth at which pregnant cows were sacrificed. The calves were ripped from the bodies of the victims and burned. The ashes were then carefully collected and placed in the *penus Vestae*, the state counterpart to the storecupboard of the family, and were used as good medicine in the city celebration of the Parilia a few days afterwards.

Upon April 19th fell the Cerealia. Ceres in later times was identified with Demeter but originally she was an Italian divinity whose character is evident from the etymological connection of the name Ceres with " *creare.*" Little is known about the ritual of the festival except the curious custom of tying lighted brands to the tails of a number of foxes which were then let loose. It has been supposed that the object in view was to secure the necessary heat for the growing crops by magical means.

Upon April 21st the festival of Parilia was held in honour of Pales, the *numen* of the shepherds' craft, a power which never became sufficiently definitely personified for its sex to be a matter of certainty and hence appears in the Latin poets as male or female indifferently. The older celebration was no doubt that of the countryside and of this both Ovid (Fasti iv., 735 foll.) and Tibullus (ii. v., 79 foll.) have given a lively picture. The steadings were decorated with leaves, branches and wreaths. The sheepfolds were purified with water and swept out with a branch while the sheep were fumigated with sulphur. Leaves of the male olive, pine, juniper or laurel, all of which crackle when burned, were thrown upon the fire and good omens for the year were deduced from the crackling. Millet and some millet cake were offered to Pales together with a pail of milk, and the shepherd, facing the east, four times repeated a prayer for the aversion of evil and for the fertility of the flock. He then washed his hands *vivo rore*, which may mean running water or perhaps more literally the morning dew to which magical properties are frequently attributed in the folklore of May-day. There followed a feast upon milk and must and in conclusion the herds were driven through the bonfire over which the shepherds also leaped, a ritual which is closely parallel to that of the Midsummer Fires familiar to students of European folklore. In the city

D

celebration of the Parilia the ashes of the calves which had been burned at the Fordicidia were mixed with the blood of the October horse[1] and then placed upon the fires making a thick smoke which was thought in some way to promote fertility.

At the Vinalia on April 23rd the wine of the previous year was ceremonially tasted and at the Robigalia on the 25th a dog was sacrificed to Robigus, the *numen* of mildew, in his grove at the fifth milestone outside Rome in order to avert the blight to which the crops, at the stage which they had now reached, might otherwise be liable

The Floralia were celebrated upon April 28th. This festival does not appear in the old calendar and the games of Flora are known to have been instituted in 238 B.C. but Flora is certainly an old Italian divinity and the rites connected with the festival, which included the letting loose in the Circus Maximus of hares and goats, animals whose fecundity and salacity have frequently earned them a place in fertility magic, and the scrambling for vetches, beans and little medals with obscene designs, have an appearance of great antiquity. It has been suggested that the older festival of Flora was a moveable feast, which

1 See below, pp. 56, 57.

varied in date with the state of the crops in any given year.   It was therefore not included in the old calendar until the date of the festival in its new form became fixed in 238 B.C.

In May, " the month of growing," the crops were now coming up and at a critical stage.   The religious ceremonies of the month are concerned with the lower world and the aversion of possible dangers.   The Lemuria, noticed in the last chapter, took place upon the 9th, 11th and 13th and upon the 21st was the Agonia Vediovis, a power whose name may mean " the opposite of Iupiter," *i.e.* the power of the underworld.   Upon May 15th took place a rite which has been inter-preted upon the analogy of similar practices in European folklore as designed to secure by magical means a sufficiency of moisture for the growing crops.   Certain puppets of human shape made of wickerwork and called Argei were thrown in to the Tiber from the Sublician Bridge by the Vestal Virgins in the presence of the *pontifices*.   It has sometimes been supposed that this ceremonial points to the existence of a primitive human sacrifice which had been mitigated by the sub-stitution of puppets for the human victims of an earlier day.   This is not however very probable. Early Italian religion appears quite free from the sacrifice of human beings and the use of puppets in similar rites of sympathetic magic is frequent in European folklore under conditions which do not necessarily presuppose substitution for human sacrifice.

Towards the end of the month took place the moveable festival of the Ambarvalia. In this the boundaries of the state were purified by a procession of purification (*lustratio*), at the head of which were driven the triple victims pig, sheep and ox (*suovetaurilia*). This lustration of the state represents the performance by the appointed officials, the Arval Brethren, on behalf of the larger community of the rites which every farmer carried out upon his own holding. Cato has preserved for us the ritual of the farmer. Three times the procession marched round the boundaries of the farm, the victims were then sacrificed and a solemn prayer, of which a portion may be quoted, was made to Mars. " Father Mars, I pray and beseech thee to be willing and propitious to me and my household and my slaves ; for the which object I have caused this threefold sacrifice to be driven round my farm and land. I pray thee keep, avert and turn from us all disease seen or unseen, all desolation, ruin, damage and unseasonable influence : I pray thee give increase to the fruits, the corn, the vines and the plantations and bring them to a prosperous issue. Keep also in safety the shepherds and their flocks and give good health and vigour to me, my house and household. To this end it is as I have said—namely for the purification and making due lustration of my farm, my land cultivated and uncultivated—that I pray thee to bless this threefold sacrifice of sucklings. O Father Mars, to this same end I pray thee to bless this threefold sacrifice of sucklings."

In this prayer the objects of the ceremonial are sufficiently indicated. The ritual has had an interesting subsequent history for the Roman Church, which inherited much of the Roman genius for effective processional ceremonial, adopted the Ambarvalia in the but slightly altered guise of the Rogation Processions and the annual practice of beating the bounds, which still survives in parts of England, can ultimately be traced back to the Roman May festival.

The months of June and July were the months of ripening and harvest ; in August the harvest was safely in and the farmer had leisure for celebrating harvest home. At the beginning of June, 7th—15th, before the work of harvest began there fell an important festival. All these days were not only *nefasti* but *religiosi* as well, that is to say not only was secular business not permissible but the days were strictly taboo and marriages, for instance, might not take place. Upon June 7th the temple of Vesta was opened; upon June 9th were the Vestalia; upon June 15th the temple was shut and the day is marked Q.S.T.D.F., "lawful when the dirt has been cleared away." Now the temple of Vesta contained the hearth of the state, the fire upon which was kept continually burning by the Vestal virgins, and the *penus Vestae*, the state counterpart to the storecupboard of the household, to which no one was allowed access except the Vestals and the *pontifex maximus*. Upon June 7th the temple was thrown open to the matrons of Rome and during the Vestalia they made procession barefoot to the temple and brought offerings of food to Vesta. The Vestals themselves made offerings of the sacred cake which it had been their duty to make from the first ears of corn ceremonially picked in May (May 7th—14th). The festival was also regarded as the holiday of bakers and millers.

Upon the 15th the temple was swept out thoroughly and the rubbish thrown into the Tiber or placed in a repository upon the Capitoline Hill. The temple was then closed and the festival was at an end, secular business becoming permissible as soon as the disposal of the rubbish had been completed. The meaning of this series of events has been explained by Warde Fowler as a symbolical and ceremonial cleansing or preparation of the storehouse of the state against its coming use at harvest time.

The main festivals of August are concerned with Consus, the *numen* of filling the storehouse (*condere*), and Ops, the wealth of harvest. Upon August 21st the Consualia were celebrated at a subterranean altar in the Circus Maximus, which was only uncovered upon this day. The subterranean altar has been thought to be a ritual survival of a primitive type of underground storehouse. The day was also marked by merrymaking; the beasts used in the harvest were given holiday and decorated and mule races were held. Four days later the associated festival of Opiconsivia was celebrated in the Regia, the king's palace which was inhabited after the fall of the monarchy by the *pontifex maximus* who had succeeded to the religious duties of the king. A similar pair of festivals occurred in December, the Consualia, December 15th, and Opalia, December 19th, and it would seem probable that the first pair in August celebrate the safe storing of the harvest while on the occasion of the second pair in December the store houses were opened and inspected to ensure that the contents were in good condition.

The corn harvest was now safely stored but there remained the vintage. The Meditrinalia, October 11th, was the autumn vintage festival at which the first must of the new vintage and the wine of the year before were ceremonially tasted. In October too (October 15th) fell what was perhaps the last of the agricultural rites of the year. A race was held for two-horsed chariots in the Campus Martius, the parade ground of the citizen army just outside the city boundary. The near horse of the winning pair was sacrificed with a spear to Mars. Its tail was cut off and carried to the Regia, where the warm blood was dripped upon the hearth. Its head was decked with cakes and the men of two neighbouring wards of Rome fought for its possession. The victors carried it off and hung up the trophy in their ward during the following year. Some of the blood of the October horse, as this victim was called, was preserved in the *penus Vestae* and used in conjunction with the ashes of the calves burned at the Fordicidia at the city celebration of the Parilia in the following April. The corn spirit is sometimes represented as a horse in European folklore, races are a constant feature of popular fertility festivals and the fight for the possession of a relic which ensures luck for the coming year is fairly common in all parts of the world.[1] It would therefore seem reasonable to suppose that the general character of this festival is that of the magical promotion of fertility.

From the equinox to the winter solstice was the season of ploughing and sowing ; respite from toil upon the farm and an opportunity for festival came first at the winter solstice. The Saturnalia, December 17th, the forerunner of our Christmas celebrations was marked by the interchange of presents between friends and the domestic merry-making of master and man. Some of the accompaniments of the feast quite probably owe their origin to later Greek influences and Saturnus came to be identified with the Greek Kronos. His Italian origin however is vindicated by his adjectival name which denotes the *numen* of sowing.

[1] The sacrifice of the Moslem Baqar 'Īd festival is in some respects singularly like that of the October horse. At Teheran a camel, gaily caparisoned, is led into a public square. " At the auspicious moment a spear in the hand of a relative of the Shah is struck into a vital spot behind the neck, and scarcely has the blood burst forth before a hundred knives are thrust into the animal by the bystanders, and in a twinkling the carcase is cut up, each quarter of the city striving to get a portion which may be kept for luck during the succeeding year." Crooke, *Herklot's Islam in India*, p. 216.

The respite from hard work in the fields lasted until the spring sowing began (about February 7th) and the Italian countryside embraced the opportunity with a number of festivals of rustic merrymaking. The last in the series was the Paganalia, January 24th to 26th, which takes its name from the *pagi* or local groups of homesteads. As before remarked the early Italians were not a people who lived in villages but in isolated farms; these however were grouped in local districts called *pagi*, analogous to the parishes of the Celtic parts of rural England. The Paganalia was a sowing festival and the powers invoked were Ceres and Earth. The motive of the ceremonies was to preserve the seed already sown in the autumn and to assist the spring sowing which was now at hand.

The last month of the Roman year, February, looked backward to the past year and to its dead. The Parentalia of February 13th to 22nd there has already been occasion to mention. *Februum* means an instrument of purification and the whole month was considered unlucky and of a gloomy character. Upon February 15th fell one of the most curious and difficult of all Roman festivals, which thanks to its accidental association with Iulius Caesar is also one of the most

celebrated.   The Lupercalia were celebrated at a
cave called the Lupercal upon the Palatine Hill.
A sacrifice of goats and a dog was made together
with an offering of the sacred cake made by the
Vestals from the first fruits of the previous year's
harvest. Two youths of high rank belonging to
the two *collegia* of *Luperci* were smeared with
the bloody knife of the sacrifice, the blood was
wiped off with wool dipped in milk and the youths
were made to laugh. They then put on the skins
of the goats, which had been sacrificed and ran
round the Palatine Hill, striking all women, whom
they met with strips of skin of the victims of the
sacrifice, which they carried in their hands.
These strips were regarded as *februa*, instruments
of purification, and the circuit of the Palatine
had the character of a lustration. The beating
had also the magical effect of stimulating fertility
and to be struck by the *Luperci* was a sovereign
remedy for the barren.

The meaning and origin of these rites had been
lost in antiquity and there was doubt even in the
Augustan age as to which deities were honoured
in the festival. The goats were sacrificed to
Faunus and the purificatory strips of skin were
associated with Iuno. The name *Luperci*, which
may mean " the warders off of wolves," and the

magical value attached to the skin of the sacrosanct animal have an air of great antiquity. On the other hand, the smearing rite is Greek in appearance rather than Latin. Indeed it is probable that the difficulties of detail will continue to give rise to conjecture and discussion but the general character of the festival as a magical purification combined with the promotion of fertility is generally admitted.[1]

With February we have reached the close of the Roman year and our brief survey of the principal fixed festivals of the old calendar has at least sufficed to illustrate the pre-occupation of this early Roman religion with the processes of agriculture and the well-being of flocks, herds and crops. That this should be the case is not surprising for the society, the needs of which it was called upon to meet, was a community of peasant farmers. Their religion, it will have been noticed, is essentially practical and the festivals are arranged with the practical end in view of taking all requisite and proper means to protect the crops and herds from danger of every kind and to

---

[1] It is reasonable to suppose, with Deubner and Warde Fowler, that no single explanation will account for all the ceremonies of the Lupercalia, because although they may have very early assumed the form in which we know them, they represent nevertheless the last stage of a long previous development in which various elements of quite different origin have been combined.

secure their increase and multiplication. It will also be noticed how seldom there has been occasion in the course of our survey to mention any member of the Graeco-Roman pantheon.

To the discussion of this point, we shall return later.

LECTURE IV

THE Calendar, which has provided us with an outline of the agricultural festivals of the year, is of course a state document. It represents the rules laid down by the state for the observance of certain festivals by and on behalf of the whole community. But in character many of those festivals are ceremonies of the farm adapted to a larger social group. Thus the official lustration of the Ambarvalia is simply the farmer's ritual described by Cato, except that the process is applied to the territory of the whole community instead of to the property of an individual and is carried out by state officials and not by the owner of the property. In fact the early religion of Rome consists of the repetition upon a larger scale of the rites of the household and the farm.

The question naturally arises as to why the state established a religion or why it was necessary to organise for the larger community a series of religious observances modelled upon those of its constituent social units. Now the note of modern religions is strongly individualistic; they are concerned with the relationship of the individual to the divine. But the early religion both of Greeks and Romans in this respect shows a marked difference. Religion for these peoples was primarily social, and this was peculiarly true of the Romans with their markedly strong corporate feeling. Speaking broadly, the significance of an individual consisted in his membership of a family, household or political community. The welfare of the family and of all its members depended upon the maintenance of right relations with the spiritual powers concerned in its existence and activities. Similarly the welfare of the larger community depended upon the maintenance of peace (*pax*) with the spiritual powers and it was incumbent upon the responsible authority, just as it was the duty of the *pater familias* within the family, to prescribe and enforce the necessary measures to secure this essential condition. In consequence *ius divinum*, religious law, is an essential and inseparable part of the civil law of the constitution. This may be observed in the recorded examples of the foundation of colonies in historical times. In such cases it was provided that as soon as the new state had been founded its *ius divinum*, *i.e.*, the regulations as to its religious calendar, ritual and priesthood should be drawn up.

The house had its secular and spiritual boundaries; the limits of the farm were guarded by Lares and Terminus and their whole circuit was annually sanctified by processional purification. Similarly the city was enclosed by a spiritual boundary, which was annually purified in the Amburbium and the territory of the state underwent lustration which was still symbolically carried out, when Roman territory became too extended for circumambulation, in the Ambarvalia. When a colony was founded a furrow was drawn round the proposed site by a bronze plough drawn by a white ox and a white cow. The sods were turned inwards to form the line of the wall and the furrow constituted the spiritual counterpart to the secular boundary of the city fortifications. The bronze plough may indeed be a ritual survival from the Bronze Age for this ceremony is older than the Etruscan influences to which it is sometimes attributed. There is evidence that in the Bronze Age the people of the *Terremare* already marked out their future settlements with the furrow made by a bronze plough.

The line traced by the ploughshare constituted the *pomerium*, the ideal boundary of the city.

The lustration of the city followed its line and within it lived the divine as well as the human inhabitants of the city. The Romans of historical times divided their gods into *di indigetes*, aboriginal deities, and *di novensides*, the gods who settled later in Rome. With the exception of Mars, whose altar lay outside the *pomerium* on the drill ground of the Campus Martius, the *di indigetes* were worshipped inside the *pomerium* while the seats of worship of the later adopted gods lay outside.

The *pomerium* then formed an invisible spiritual rampart round the community which was broken only at the gates. Gaps had necessarily to be left in the sacred barrier for the passage of secular traffic and communication consequently when the site of an intended gateway was reached the plough was lifted and a gap was left unhallowed by the furrow. Hence gateways constituted the weak point in the spiritual as well as in the material defences of a city, just as the door was a point of danger in the house. It was for this reason that in the ceremonies of purification the gates of the town demanded special attention and that at Iguvium, for instance, as we know from inscriptions, special sacrifices were offered at each of the three gates.

E

The life of the state, like the life of the household, centred round a hearth and a storecupboard. The circular temple of Vesta contained the state hearth upon which the fire might never be allowed to go out except upon March the first. Upon that date, at the end of the old year and at the beginning of the new, the fire was ceremonially extinguished and fresh fire was kindled by the antique method of rubbing two dry sticks together. This of course belongs to the class of rite, which M. van Gennep has labelled *rites de passage ;* at the moment of passing from the old year to the new the fire of the state, upon which prosperity depended, was rekindled and thereby given new vigour for the coming year. The cult of the household hearth was in the charge of the women of the family ; analogously the hearth of the state was tended by the Vestal virgins, who were originally the daughters of the king, who stood to the political community in the same relation as the *pater familias* to the household. In the household the daughters were concerned with the care of the storecupboard and the cooking ; it was therefore the duty of the Vestals to make the sacrificial salt cake (*mola salsa*) and to keep the contents of the *penus Vestae* to which only the *pontifex maximus,* besides themselves, had access.

The state worship of Vesta is therefore nothing more than an adaptation to the larger community of household ritual. In one particular the lines of subsequent development in state and household respectively diverged. In family worship the Penates seem to have increased in importance at the expense of Vesta ; in part this may have been due to their mistaken association with the ancestors of the family. In the worship of the state however the opposite is true. The Penates of the state are insignificant ; their abode is even called the *penus Vestae* and it is Vesta who supplies the significant figure.

The house, it will be remembered, was under the protection of the *numen* of its door, Ianus. This cult also the state took over and an archway or gate at the north east side of the Forum was the seat of its corresponding *numen*. As a state deity Ianus, intelligibly enough, developed a new, wider and more abstract significance. Doors both open and shut ; consequently Ianus is alternatively the opener or the closer, cult titles (*Patulci Cloesi*) which are found already in the Saliaric hymn. For this reason when art was later called upon to represent his image, he was portrayed with two faces (*bifrons*). The god of openings is naturally the god of beginnings and a series of cult titles follow the natural lines of development from this idea. As Consevius Ianus controlled the beginnings of human life; he was the god of the first hour of the day, of the first month after the winter solstice and of the first day of the month. In the liturgy of prayer his name came first and that of Vesta last in the order of divine powers invoked.

It has already been noticed that the king stands to the community in the same relation as the *pater familias* to the household. Within the family the *pater familias* had complete authority, though by custom he was expected in important matters to consult a family council; the king similarly was required by custom to seek the advice in secular matters of the aristocratic council, the senate, in spiritual matters of the board of *pontifices*. The reason why the members of this board of religious experts should have been called " bridge builders " remains completely obscure. After the fall of the monarchy and throughout the history of the republic the college of *pontifices* represented the highest spiritual authority in the state and their chairman, the *pontifex maximus*, inherited the greater part of the royal prerogatives in matters of religion.

The *ius divinum*, it will be remembered, was

not different in nature from civil law of which it
was indeed a part.   No mystic vocation was
therefore required of a *pontifex* but knowledge
of religious law and wisdom in administration.
It followed that membership of the college of
pontifices was no bar to secular office and could
in fact be held simultaneously with the highest
magistracies of the state.

The *pontifices* held office for life.   When a
vacancy occurred the college co-opted a new
member. In dress they were distinguished by the
toga with the purple stripe, the religious significance of which we have already noticed in connection with the dress of childhood, and the tall
conical hat (*apex*) like that worn by the *Salii*.

The president of the board, *pontifex maximus*
lived in the Regia or royal palace. It was he who
appointed the Vestal virgins, the *rex sacrorum*
and the *flamines*. He controlled the administration of the state religion and inasmuch as all
legal administration of a semi-religious character,
e.g. burials, wills, adoptions or change of status
from Patrician to Plebeian fell within his purview,
he exercised great authority also over the private
lives of citizens.

The *rex sacrorum*, whose title, like that of the
Archon Basileus at Athens, indicates a con-

stitutional survival from the monarchy, inherited
some of the executive religious functions of the
king. He was appointed for life upon the nomination of the *pontifex maximus*. He was a religious
official with certain definite executive duties but
without administrative powers. His office implied
active personal contact with sacred things and it
therefore conferred sacrosanctity upon the person
of its holder. An equally logical result of its
sacred character was a disability to hold secular
office.

A similar disability for similar reasons attached
to the office of *flamen*, kindler, *i.e.* officiating
priest. There were three of these priesthoods
which descended from very early times—that of
Iupiter (*Flamen Dialis*), that of Mars (*Flamen
Martialis*) and that of Quirinus, the form of
Mars peculiar to the early settlement of the
Quirinal hill (*Flamen Quirinalis*). The order of
their precedence was that in which their names
have been given and of the three the *Flamen
Dialis* was the first in dignity and importance.
The great antiquity, social importance and
sanctity of his office is shown by the multitude of
taboos with which his life and that of his wife and
children was hedged. He might not for instance
touch a goat or a dog, eat beans, wheat or leavened

bread, cut his hair or nails with an iron knife or wear any knot or ring upon his person. The numerous rules of avoidance which attached to his office in fact so circumscribed his life with inconvenience that in historical times it became difficult to find persons who were willing to fill the post and for many years before the reforms of Augustus this, the greatest and oldest of the priesthoods, fell into abeyance.

The *fetiales* were a board of twenty members of some politico-religious importance whose province was that of Rome's relations with foreign communities, which of course included their divine as well as their human inhabitants. It will be evident that the regular observance of their duties must have exercised a strong influence upon the development of international fair-dealing and the idea, in which indeed their existence is rooted, that the relations between communities are governed by equity (*fas*). The ceremonial of the declaration of war or peace and that of the making of treaties was performed by them.

In early times the *fetiales* carried out their duties in pairs though it appears that later two pairs might be sent out in co-operation. One of the two members of a mission was called *verbenarius* because he carried a bunch of herbs, which at once served as a badge of their inviolable office and at the same time acted as a magical prophylactic against the supernatural dangers to be encountered in a foreign country. The other was called " ratifying father of the Roman people " (*pater patratus populi Romani*), *i.e.*, plenipotentiary representative of the Roman state. In the case of a dispute arising with another community the mission advanced to the borders of the state in question and there the *pater patratus* called Iupiter to witness the justice of the complaints or claims of Rome. This statement was repeated to the first individual who was encountered after crossing the frontier, to the sentinel at the city gate and finally to the magistrate and people in their market place. At Rome the citizen army was mobilised and thirty days' interval allowed. If the ultimatum expired without satisfaction being accorded to the Roman claim, war was then declared. The *pater patratus* once more advanced to the frontier and hurled across it a ritual spear of primitive type (a wooden lance the point of which had been hardened in the fire), which had been dipped in blood. This symbolical action constituted a declaration of war. At the making of treaties the *pater patratus* also

acted as the representative of Rome. He struck
the sacrificial victim with the sacred flint and
gave sanction to the oath of ratification by in-
voking Iupiter to strike down the Roman people
even as the victim had been struck, if they did
not observe the oath which had been taken.

It will be noticed that under the Republic there
is a marked separation of administrative and
executive religious functions but this was not
probably the case under the monarchy. In all
probability the *rex* not only enjoyed the administrative authority which passed to the *pontifex
maximus* but performed also those duties of active
participation in the ritual of cult which fell
subsequently to the *rex sacrorum*. He may also
have been the chairman of the board of *augures*.
According to tradition these had originally been
three in number until Numa by adding two
further members brought them up to five. We
know that in 300 B.C. the board had four members
and this becomes explicable if it is supposed that
the king had been *ex-officio* on the board but that
no arrangements to fill his place had been made
after the expulsion of Tarquin. Similarly the
king's seat upon the board of *pontifices* was said
to have been left vacant. It must be confessed
however that there are good grounds for believing

that Livy was right in thinking that the numbers of these corporations should properly be three or a multiple of three. He accounts for there being only four augurs at the date mentioned by supposing that two had died. In 300 B.C. a law was passed increasing the numbers of both colleges and asserting the eligibility of Plebeians to membership. The total was eventually fixed at fifteen under Sulla's scheme for the general re-organisation of the magistracies and religious boards and was finally increased to sixteen by Iulius Caesar.

The augurs enjoyed no powers of initiative in the administration or celebration of cult. Their function was that of skilled interpreters to explain the signs vouchsafed by heaven upon occasions of importance, *e.g.*, at the consecration of priests, the blessing of the farms or the blessing of the people at the close of a successful war. The actual right of observation of the signs (*spectio*) was confined to the secular magistrate. The augur's duty was limited to giving expert advice as to the meaning of signs so observed. The augur's interpretation, however, was final. In consequence the office conferred considerable power in promoting or prohibiting political action. Owing to the conception of the augur as a wise expert

rather than an official of any especial holiness,
there were no religious taboos or disabilities
attaching to the office and it could be held
in conjunction with the highest secular
magistracies.

Augurs wore the *toga praetexta* and carried as
a badge of their office a curved wand (*lituus*)
with which they marked out the *templum* or
defined area in which the signs were to be manifested and observed. Livy's account of the
inauguration of Numa gives a picture of the
traditional procedure.[1] Numa was led on to the
Capitol from which there was a commanding
view over the city of Rome and its territory.
He was seated upon a stone with his face to the
south. The augur with covered head took his
seat to the left of the king with the *lituus* in his
right hand. After surveying the city and territory
of Rome and offering up a prayer, he then
marked out the *templum* from east to west and
defined the area to the south of its axis as being
the Right, that to the north the Left. The king
thus faced the area in which lucky signs might
be observed. The augur then shifted his *lituus*
to his left hand, laid his right upon Numa's head,
and prayed " If it is right that this Numa

[1] Livy, I, 18.

Pompilius, whose head I hold, be king in Rome, allow us to see unmistakable signs within the boundaries marked." He then stated what signs he wished to be sent.

The Romans distinguished between *auspicia impetriva*, in which a sign was demanded, and *auspicia oblativa*, signs which are sent unsought, generally of course portents of evil omen. The right of observing public auspices of the first kind was exclusively reserved for secular magistrates and the *pontifex maximus*, though the skilled services of an augur as assessor might be desirable and even necessary. Any citizen and *a fortiori* any magistrate could report the observance of a chance omen.

It should of course be realised that Roman augury is hardly true divination in the sense of an attempt to pry into the secrets of the future ; it is rather of the nature of a test as to whether a course of action, which has already been decided upon by the state or its official representative, is approved by the divine powers. The conditions of the test are laid down and an answer is necessarily obtained, for it is not information but a simple " yes " or " no " which is demanded.

It has generally been held that both *augurium* and *auspicium* are etymologically connected with

auis " a bird " and that the oldest method of
Roman augury was that of the observation of the
flight of birds. The importance attached in the
early Republic to the signs afforded by lightning
is due no doubt to Etruscan influence and to
Etruria the Romans owed the elaboration, if not
the origin, of the method of the examination of
the entrails of the victim of sacrifice. I am still
inclined to think that the germ of this method
was already present in early Roman religious
custom before Etruscan influences became dominant and is in fact to be found in the practice
of examining the liver of the victim of sacrifice
in order to make sure that it was healthy and
normal and therefore a fit and proper offering to
be made. A comparison of the models of livers,
charts as it were to guide interpretation, which
have been found both in Etruria and Babylon,
has suggested a Mesopotamian origin for the
elaborate form of this art. There is however a
considerable gap of time and space to be bridged
between the two civilisations, even though we
may safely admit that the Etruscans probably
came to Italy from Asia Minor, and the hypothesis
of a parallel but independent development is not
perhaps to be excluded.

The college of augurs became more and more a

political body exercising political influence in Rome, which they were therefore naturally unwilling to leave.   The methods of divination in the field in practice became limited to the examination of entrails and the observation of how the chickens, which were kept for that purpose, took their food. These methods had the practical advantage of being simple and expeditious.   The chickens were carried with the army in coops by the *pullarius*, who had charge of them, and prudence dictated that they should be adequately starved to ensure that at the right time they would fall eagerly upon their food, which was the desired sign of heaven's approval.

Throughout its history the Roman state discouraged prophecy and private unauthorised divination.   The Marsian magicians, upon whom Ennius pours scorn and the Sabellian wise women of Horace were no doubt consulted by private persons but the attitude of the state towards them was as definitely hostile as it was towards the Chaldeans and Oriental magicians who succeeded in more sophisticated times to the position which was earlier occupied by members of the less civilised tribes of Italy.   There is one partial exception.   Upon critical occasions when portents occurred for which the *pontifices* were unable to prescribe a remedy, recourse might be had for advice to the *haruspices* of Etruria, who enjoyed a great prestige as the masters of an ancient magical lore.   Such reference however was under strict control and could only be made after the expressed decision of the senate that it was necessary.[1]

[1] Prodigia, portenta ad Etruscos haruspices, si senatus iussit, deferunto. Cicero, *De Leg*, II, 9.

LECTURE V

CERTAIN features of early Roman religion will
now be clear which the organisation of religion
by the state are likely to accentuate. In the first
place the worship of *numina* leaves no room for
a personal tie between the worshipper and the
object of worship. The latter is indeed an object
of awe and reverence but not of love. It has
neither like passions nor like sympathies with
man. In fact the religious duties of which the
feeling of awe has inspired the performance,
constitute the human side of a contract. The
whole conception of religion is strongly tinged
with legal conceptions.

This contractual view of religious obligation
inevitably helps to widen the gap between the
individual and the object of his worship. The
essential duty upon the human side is to secure
the performance of the necessary rites, at the
proper time, at the proper place, and with
exactly accurate formulae. The least mistake in
any detail of the performance renders the whole

nugatory. From this conception of the nature of religious duty it follows that the efficacy of ceremonies depends upon knowing how they should rightly be performed. Religion is therefore an expert affair and the performance of active religious duties is left to the experts. The layman's share in religious observance is mainly negative, *i.e.*, to abstain from any action which might hinder, interfere with or vitiate the expert's performance. "Not till the advent of the Sibylline books and the *Graecus ritus* did the people take an active part in the state religion; their duty was merely to abstain from disturbance during the performance of sacred rites. 'Feriis jurgia amovento' is the only reference in Cicero's imaginary sketch of the *ius divinum* to the conduct of the citizen on festival days."[1]

It will be observed that the action of the state in taking over, organising, and defining religious obligation in the interests of the community and regularising its administration through properly constituted officials of the state is a logical consequence of this general view of the nature of religion. Discipline of course it exacted and thus helped to develope an important side of Roman character but clearly from a moral and

---

[1] Warde Fowler, *Rel. Exp.*, p. 173.   Cicero, *De Leg.*, ii, 8, 19.

F

religious point of view it has its defects. The
active duties of religion and with them inevitably
all sense of individual responsibility are transferred
from the layman to the expert. Further the
intense emphasis upon the exact correctness of
ritual necessarily involved a rigid conservatism
in traditional form. It is obvious, however, that
in course of time the meaning of rites will become
obliterated. The words of the hymns traditionally
handed down become a mere hocus pocus to the
layman, who no longer speaks the language in
which they were written, and even the performer
will no longer understand the formulae which
he recites. Indeed in the first century B.C.
hardly a word of the *axamenta*, which they
chanted, can have been intelligible to the *Salii*.

Again both the caution natural to minds of a
legal bias and the tendency of experts to enhance
the importance of their science by elaboration
led to the development of an arid formalism.
Long lists of *indigitamenta* were drawn up defining
the appropriate *numina* concerned with every
detailed action of human life and religion was
wrapped in an artificial complexity which was as
elaborately meticulous and as unintelligible to
the layman as that of legal documents.[1]

[1] See below, p. 114.

The result of the organisation of religion by the
state upon the lines indicated was that at a
particular and that an early stage of social
and political development the Roman religious
system was stereotyped. Its practice was widely
removed from life in the sense of any mental
activity or personal need of the individual.
Further this gulf between religion and the needs
of life was bound to grow wider until there
was hardly a real point of contact. For the
religion of Numa was devised to provide for
the needs of a small agricultural society whose
only interests were the prospects of the harvest
and of the summer campaign. It consisted
of a perfectly rigid system, which left no room
for development or expansion beyond the mere
elaboration of detail. But Rome could not
and did not in fact remain a small community
of peasant farmers. New needs inevitably arose
from changed social and economic conditions
and these a rigid system drawn up to supply
needs of a particular and very limited character
was unable to meet.

How the new needs were met will be discussed
later. Here it suffices to point out that polytheism
is not exclusive. It does not deny the existence
or validity of other men's gods. Nor is there

anything repugnant to Roman religious ideas in the feeling that if circumstances arise, which are not provided for by the invocations or rites of the native religion, help may be sought elsewhere and the state may legitimately supplement its religious system by the adoption of foreign rites.

The result however of the introduction and adoption of foreign cults was the introduction also of foreign religious ideas and the old religion was strangled by the new influences. It was inevitable that a ritual devised for peasant farmers should become more and more divorced from the actualities of life in an imperial and cosmopolitan community. As the language changed, the antiquated forms of its liturgy became less and less intelligible. Inevitably the newer elements came to bulk more important than the old. But further the foreign rites with which the state cult was supplemented were fundamentally in-consistent with the older order of native worship. They were antagonistic in essence because the roots of their origin lay in religious conceptions quite different to those from which the worship of *numina* derived.

Before passing on to trace the history of this development, it may be worth while to consider a little more closely the objects of early Roman worship. The following list, copied from the pages of Wissowa, enumerates in alphabetical order the names of divine powers belonging to the religion of Numa. Opposite each name is given the festivals with which it is peculiarly associated.

ANNA PERENNA Festival, March 15th.

CARMENTA . Carmentalia, January 11th, 15th.

CARNA . . Festival, June 1st.

CERES . . Cerealia, April 19th.

CONSUS . . Consualia, August 21st and December 15th.

DIVA ANGERONA Divalia, December 21st.

FALACER . .

FAUNUS . . Lupercalia, February 15th.

FLORA . . Florifertum (?).

FONS . . Fontinalia, October 13th.

FURRINA . . Furrinalia, July 25th.

IANUS . . Agonium, January 9th ; Tigillum sororium, October 1st.

IUPITER . . The Ides of every month. Vinalia, April 23rd and August 19th ; Meditrinalia. October 11th ; Poplifugium, July 5th, Festival on December 23rd.

LARENTA . Larentalia, December 23rd.

LARES . . Compitalia.

LEMURES ? . Lemuria, May 9th, 11th, and 13th.

LIBER . . Liberalia, March 17th.

MARS . . Equirria, February 27th and March 14th ; Festival on March 1st ; Agonium Martiale, March 17th ; Quinquatrus, March 19th ; Tubilustrium, March 23rd (and ? 23rd May) ; October Horse, October 15th ; Armilustrium, October 19th. Ambarvalia.

MATER MATUTA	Matralia, June 11th.
NEPTUNUS .	Neptunalia, July 23rd.
OPS . .	Opiconsivia, August 25th; Opalia, December 19th.
PALES, PALATUA	Parilia, April 21st.
POMONA . .	
PORTUNUS .	Portunalia, August 17th.
QUIRINUS .	Quirinalia, February 17th.
ROBIGUS . .	Robigalia, April 25th.
SATURNUS .	Saturnalia, December 17th.
TELLUS . .	Fordicidia, April 15th, Feriae Sementivae.
TERMINUS .	Terminalia, February 23rd.
VEIOVIS . .	Agonium, May 21st.
VESTA . .	Vestalia, June 9th.
VOLCANUS .	Volcanalia, August 23rd.
VOLTURNUS .	Volturnalia, August 27th.

The feature in this list which will first strike a reader who is familiar with classical literature, is its omissions. Very few of the gods and goddesses with whom classical literature has made him familiar figure in it. There is no mention for example of Diana, Minerva or Apollo. Further the names of gods, which he recognises, appear to denote powers possessing more limited functions or functions different to those which are associated with them in Latin literature. Liber for instance is not the god of wine but a fertility power. Iupiter to judge by his festivals is primarily a vine god. Our reader will miss Iupiter Optimus

Maximus ; Mars not Iupiter appears to be the national god. On the other hand there are a great many names like Falacer or Furrina which are unintelligible to him and in fact would equally have puzzled Cicero or Ovid.

The names upon our list it will be noticed fall into three main classes. Firstly there are names which express some natural object or thing : *e.g.* Fons, fountain ; Terminus, boundary ; Tellus, earth ; Ianus, door ; Vesta, hearth. Here we have clearly an inheritance from animism ; the worship that is to say of the spirits or forces thought to be resident in these objects.

Secondly there are adjectival names formed from the name of some object or from a verb expressing some function or activity, *e.g.* Saturnus " of sowing." Clearly this represents a further development of animistic thought. Earth has some power in it, which makes it function, so has " boundary " or " door." The early Roman went further and believed that in any activity there is an incalculable force which makes it work. Saturnus is the force which makes sowing effective. *Numen*, as we have seen, is connected with *nuere* " to will."

Thirdly there are gods who seem in some degree to possess personality : Iupiter, Mars, Quirinus.

The religion then of Numa represents a
transition stage from numinism or animism to
deism, from the worship of functional powers
which have neither sex nor personality to that
of divine persons. But here it may be asked
whether we have any right to assume this order
of development and suppose that the gods of
our third class are the result of a process of the
gradual personalisation of *numina*. In justification
it may be pleaded that while the process by which
a personality may be developed out of the
indeterminate concept of an impersonal force
is intelligible, the reverse process is more
difficult to imagine. Further it is perhaps
possible in the case of Vesta and Ianus to
watch such a development actually taking place.
The names of these two divinities place them
in our first category. Vesta is the *numen* of
the hearth, Ianus the *numen* of the door. The
worship of both lived as long as paganism
survived. Vesta may be said partially to have
developed personality. In Cicero's time the fire
on the hearth still *was* Vesta but undoubtedly
his contemporaries thought of Vesta as a goddess
of hearth and home possessing personality and
sex ; to the end however she remained so far
true to her original character that her temple

never contained an image.   Ianus was originally the door.   The place of his public worship remained an archway in the Forum.   But Ianus became the god of beginnings ;   he lost, if we may put it so, the limitations of his doorness. He was represented in art by the statue of a male figure with two faces and a Roman of the first century B.C., would certainly have understood by Ianus a divine male personality.

The roots then of Roman religion appear to lie in animism or the worship of powers which exist in objects or activities.   If this is so, certain negative conclusions follow which are so important that they will bear repetition.   Firstly it is clear that the once popular Aryan theory breaks down completely in the case of Roman religion.   Roman objects of worship cannot originate in personifications of the thunder, the storm, the dawn or the night, if they are not personifications at all.   Abstract functional powers refuse to fall into line with the hypothetical system of nature worship attributed to the Aryan ancestors of the peoples who speak dialects of the Indo-European language.   Roman mythology cannot be " highly figurative conversation about the weather " for the best of reasons ;   there is no Roman mythology.   *Numina* have no personality. Their worshippers were a practical and unspeculative people; they were interested only in the activity of these powers; they therefore made up no stories about them. For similar reasons it is obvious that Roman religion cannot have its origin in the worship of the stars.

Secondly none of the various forms of Euhemerism can explain the origin of Roman religion. Euhemerus first promulgated the rationalist theory that gods arose from the grateful memory of the beneficence of great men who thus became deified by posterity. But the memory of a John Nicholson, whose personality gave rise to a god worshipped on the North Western Frontier of India, could not give rise to the worship of an impersonal *numen*.

Modern Euhemerists sometimes search for a universal source of religion in ancestor-worship and claim that it is everywhere the ultimate origin of human religious development. Whatever may be the case elsewhere, their theory is not true of Roman religion. It is difficult to derive " door," Ianus, or even " of sowing," Saturnus, from a dead ancestor. A Roman *gens* had often an ancestral connection with some particular religious cult but its members, unlike those of the Greek γένος, did not claim a common descent from a god. Further, if we may be allowed to emphasise the point once more, there is no evidence for the individualisation of the dead in early Rome. The title of the collective dead is plural : " Telluri ac Dis Manibus " ran the formula by which a Roman general devoted the enemy to the nether powers. No word for the singular spirit of a dead man exists and later usage, which does not appear to be earlier than the first century B.C., has to employ the plural *Manes* for the spirit of an individual. Rites at Roman tombs do not appear to be in a strict sense acts of worship but rather acts of commemoration and until Greek eschatology was introduced into Rome there are no traces of theories about an after life.

Thirdly we have seen that thanks to the abstract nature of the objects of worship and the practical character of the worshipper, there is no Roman mythology. There is similarly no Roman cosmogony, for the Roman indulged in no speculations as to how the objects of his worship came into being. *Numina* have no physical relation among themselves nor do they stand in any physical relation to their worshippers. The Greek Zeus is the father of gods and men ; the Roman Iupiter is neither.

To this it will be objected that Roman deities
are often addressed as father or mother. Iupiter
himself is Dies Pater and Tellus is Tellus Mater.
It remains true, however, that until Greek
mythology, with its system of a divine family of
inter-related gods, was introduced there is no hint
of any similar inter-relation between Roman
objects of worship. It is possible that the use of
father and mother in invocation need not imply
a physical relationship at all, but be merely a
propitiatory mode of address, as when a Russian
should address his master as " Little Father."

Fourthly some students have attempted to find
in early Roman religion a number of grouped
pairs of wedded deities. The foundation of their
argument however is in Graeco-Roman mythology. If we are right in thinking that Roman
gods were developed from *numina* and that a
numen has no personality and therefore no sex,
we shall be unable to agree with them. Now the
indeterminate character of the sex of the objects
of early Roman worship is shown by the caution
of liturgical formulae in later times. If *numina*
possessed sex, it was not known which it was, and
hence *Sive mas sive femina*, " whether male or
female " was added to the invocation to make sure
that it reached the right quarter. Pales, a rustic

power which remained uninfluenced by Greek mythology, is indifferently masculine or feminine in the Augustan poets.

The chief support of the theory of the wedded pairs of divinities rests upon certain phrases which are known to have occurred in sacred formulae such as Lua Saturni, Salacia Neptuni, Virites Quirini, Nerio Martis. It has been suggested that these words, feminine in gender, represent female counterparts or wives of the male powers with whom they are associated and it is quite true that later Roman mythology knew a story of the wooing of Nerio by Mars. But, owing to the untrustworthy nature of the evidence of mythology for early Roman belief, this is not in itself conclusive and there is evidently an inherent difficulty in reconciling a primitive cult of wedded pairs of deities with numinism, which upon other grounds we have been led to regard as the most probable origin of Roman religion. Nor is it by any means clear that these feminine words originally represented female personalities. There is reason to believe rather that they may be abstract qualities. Nerio for instance appears to be equivalent to *virtus* and Cerus, Cerfia, Cerfus, mentioned in the formula below, seem to be connected etymologically with *creare* and to have something of the same meaning as *genius*. Although formulae of this kind indisputably belong to the religion of Numa, they probably belong to its latest stages and represent the product of sacerdotal elaboration. Such must be the explanation of a phrase like Praestita Cerfia Cerfi Martii, " protecting spirit (feminine) of the spirit (masculine) of Mars."[1]

The observations, which a list of the objects of worship of early Roman religion has suggested, are not without a certain negative interest to students of comparative religion. They confirm the wisdom of that caution, which now prevails among students of social anthropology in contrast to their predecessors, in adopting any single hypothesis which is to explain the origin of every human religious system. To several of the master-keys which were once popular, Aryan nature worship, ancestor worship, the worship of wedded pairs of fertility deities, Roman religion refuses to yield.

There is yet another difficult question. Did the early Romans worship animals ? Again if we are right about the character of *numina*, it is difficult to reconcile with their worship a theriomorphic conception of divinity. I am personally

[1] A discussion of this difficult matter will be found in Warde Fowler, *Religious Experience*, pp. 149, 481, foll. Cf. Wissowa, p. 134.

of opinion that the direct worship of animals is
a great deal less frequent than is sometimes
supposed nor in the particular case of Roman
religion do I know of any evidence of which the
early existence of animal worship is a necessary
consequence, though there are, it is true, facts
of which the theory of animal worship supplies
a plausible explanation. It is certain that Mars
was very early associated with the wolf and the
woodpecker not only by the Romans but by the
Italic peoples in general. The tribal names of
Hirpini, " the wolf men," or Picentini, " the
woodpecker men," may be quoted in support of
the early importance of these creatures and may
be compared with tribal appellations like Marsi
or Marrucini, which are clearly taken from Mars.
At the same time I know of no traces of the actual
cult of a wolf or of a woodpecker with the possible
exception of an Italian oracle at Tiora Matiene
at which a woodpecker was said in some way to
be concerned with the delivery of the responses.
Dionysius of Halicarnassus, who had not himself
been there, was told that the woodpecker performed the same functions as the doves at Dodona.
Unfortunately, though from the time of Herodotus
onwards there have been numerous theories
about the doves of Dodona, we are in fact

completely in the dark as to what they were and what they did.

For myself I consider it more probable that the wolf and woodpecker gained their religious importance from becoming associated with Mars rather than that they were originally themselves independent objects of worship. The grounds of such association are not difficult to imagine. Both are wild creatures appropriate to the wild god and in addition to its martial appearance, which Plutarch noticed, the woodpecker is qualified for association with Mars in his other aspect of the god of spring and growth, for throughout Europe it has been regarded as a bird which brings the rain.

The list of objects of worship suggested that the Religion of Numa was at a transition stage from numinism to deism and in the third class of powers, which can certainly be called gods, stand three of whom something must be said. Although they were not worshipped in temples nor represented by images in human shape, Iupiter, Mars and Quirinus are already divine personalities when first we hear of them. They occupied in this early religion the prominence which Iupiter, Iuno and Minerva afterwards enjoyed under the Etruscan kings. To them were

attached the three most ancient priesthoods the
offices of *Flamen Dialis*, *Flamen Martialis* and
Flamen Quirinalis.

About Quirinus very little is known. In later
days he was identified with Romulus but he seems
originally to have been the peculiar deity, corresponding to Mars, of the settlement upon the
Quirinal Hill. No doubt he was incorporated
into the Roman religious system as a consequence
of the political amalgamation of the two communities. It would appear however that he was
completely dwarfed by his greater double, Mars.
Of the three great *flamines* that of Quirinus was
the junior and while the *Flamen Dialis* and the
Flamen Martialis were solely and completely
occupied with the cults of their respective deities,
a number of extra duties, *e.g.* the sacrifice to
Robigus, fell to the *Flamen Quirinalis*. This has
suggested that as the cult of Quirinus waned in
importance, its duties became less exacting; in
consequence the Flamen of Quirinus was enabled
to undertake extra duties connected with other
cults.

Iupiter may have been originally the *numen* of
the sky. It is certain that from a very early date
he was worshipped by all the peoples of the
Italic stock. His cult was especially connected with

G

high places and with the oak, a tree peculiarly associated with the god of lightning.[1] It was perhaps because the days of full moon provide the longest period of continuous light that the Ides were sacred to Iupiter.

In his *Roman Ideas of Deity* Warde Fowler threw out a suggestion that the worship of Iupiter may be a survival of an aboriginal monotheism to which numinism and the deities subsequently evolved from *numina* were but an accretion. Difference from so great a master of his subject is always hazardous but here we are outside historical times for which the opinion of one, who had so lived into Roman literature that almost he caught the sentiments of an ancient Roman, must always carry a peculiar authority. I confess that I do not find it very easy to accept this theory of an aboriginal monotheism, in support of which no very cogent evidence can be produced and I am inclined to doubt, if the anthropological testimony adduced in its favour, is quite so strong and trustworthy as Warde Fowler supposed.

Under the Etruscan monarchy, Iupiter became the chief guardian of the Roman state but even

1. It appears to be a fact that the oak is more liable to be struck by lightning than other trees. Upon this point Warde Fowler has collected some interesting evidence in *Roman Essays*, pp. 37, foll.

in earlier times his worship had a political aspect.
This is shown in the cult of Iupiter Latiaris, in
which members of the Latin League united.
Although our records of its celebration refer to
Republican times, when the leading part was
taken by the Roman consuls as the chief executive
magistrates of the dominant member of the
League, the character of the ritual points to a
very early origin and even suggests a survival from
a time when the participants were mainly a
pastoral people.

The ceremony took place at a grove upon the
Alban Mount, the extinct volcano which, rising
in the middle of the Latin plain, provided a city
of refuge or acropolis for the people living around
its base. The federal offerings consisted of sheep,
cheese and milk; the victims were white steers
which had not borne the yoke. The flesh of the
sacrifice was eaten in a sacramental meal which
was followed by feasting. A feature of the festival
was the practice of suspending small images,
masks, or balls (*oscilla*) to the trees. A discussion
of this and similar rites from all parts of the world
will be found in Sir James Frazer's *Golden Bough*.[1]

In Rome itself there were several very ancient

---

[1] Frazer, *The Golden Bough, Part III., The Dying God*, Note B.,
p.p. 277-285.

cults of Iupiter. As Feretrius, the god of the thunderbolt, he was worshipped at an ancient oak upon the Capitol. Other cult titles, *e.g.* Elicius or Fulmen, attest his manifestation in the lightning. As Iupiter Lapis he was worshipped as immanent in a flint, possibly a stone celt, which was kept in a shrine, hard by the oak of Iupiter Feretrius. This stone was used by the *fetiales* in the ceremonial above described and they swore *per Iovem Lapidem.* Mention may also be made of a very curious and ancient ceremony of rain-making which was called *aquaelicium.* In time of drought a procession of matrons with bare feet accompanied by the magistrates without the insignia of their office, escorted a stone, called the Lapis Manalis, from the Porta Capena to Iupiter Elicius on the Aventine, where water was ceremonially poured over it.

Clearly this is in itself a very primitive rite and was intended to cause rain by sympathetic magic. The antiquity of the procession of matrons however may perhaps be questioned. It has a Greek appearance and in fact the evidence for this feature of the ritual is derived from Petronius who is writing not of Rome but of a South Italian town.

At a very early date Iupiter became the god

who sanctioned the oath and was invoked as Deus
Fidius. He thus became the god of justice and the
power which sanctioned the observance of treaties.
Hence his worship exercised a powerful influence
upon the development of moral and political
ideas. There is no evidence, however, that
in the religion of Numa Iupiter occupied the
position, which he held later, of the chief political
deity of the Roman state. The festivals associated
with his name in the ancient calendar show him
to be primarily concerned with the cultivation
of the vine. The Vinalia April 23rd, Vinalia
Rustica August 19th, and Meditrinalia October
11th, are all sacred to the sky-god and it was his
priest, the *Flamen Dialis*, who ceremonially
plucked the first grapes at the *vindemiae auspicatio*.

Of the problems connected with Mars a very
good and clear summary will be found in
Mr. Bailey's Introduction to his edition of Ovid,
Fasti, III. To a Roman of the Augustan age
Mars was primarily the god of war and the divine
ancestor through Romulus of the Roman race.
There is evidence that before history can be said
to begin his worship was common to the majority
of the Italic peoples. That in the earliest days
of Rome he possessed a military aspect is un-
questionable. His sacred spears were kept in the

Regia, the palace of the king, and before a war the general in command entered the treasury of Mars, shook the spears and shields and called upon Mars to watch (*Mars vigila*). His dancing priests, the *Salii*, wore the full dress of the ancient Italian warrior. To Mars were sacred the ceremonies of the purification of the arms and army of the state at the beginning and at the end of the campaigning season (Armilustrium March 17th; Tubilustrium March 23rd; October Horse October 15th; Armilustrium October 19th). At the completion of each *lustrum*, or period of five years, the Roman people were purified by the threefold offering (*suovetaurilia*) and for this purpose they met under arms upon the Field of Mars, the drill ground of the citizen army. In this military aspect has been sought the explanation why until the time of Augustus Mars, though indisputably one of the *di indigetes*, was worshipped outside not inside the *pomerium*. War was not allowed inside the spiritual boundaries of the city; only in the official celebration of victory did the citizen army enter the walls in the triumphal procession to the Capitol and then only after passing under the triumphal arch which purified them from the infection of war and slaughter.

But besides this aspect of the god of war Mars has clearly another and a different character. He gave its name to the first month in the year, the season not only of campaigning but also of spring. There is reason to believe that the dance of the *Salii* was not merely a war dance but was intended magically to promote the growth of the crops. In the lustration of the farm it is to Mars that Cato addressed his prayer for the fruitfulness of his farm and he was the deity invoked in the analogous state ritual of the Ambarvalia. The hymns of the Arval Brethren call upon Mars to avert pestilence, to promote fruitfulness and to leap to the threshold.

This dual aspect of Mars in early Roman religion is not questioned but there has been considerable dispute as to which element represents his original character. Wissowa has uncompromisingly maintained that his military aspect is primary and his fertility aspect secondary. The majority, however, of serious students of Roman religion are of opinion that upon general grounds this is not probable. They point out that in early Latium the ordinary man was both farmer and soldier; armati terram exercent. Warde Fowler suggested that Silvanus, the spirit of the forest, was in origin a cult title of Mars. The spirit of the

woodland was at once the *numen* of birth and
fertility, particularly that of flocks and herds,
and was also the power which reigned in the
mysterious and dreaded forest which lay beyond
the homestead. To this wild character he would
attribute the development of the conception of
Mars as the god of violence and warfare and the
exclusion of the worship of Mars outside the
pomerium he would explain as an heritage from
Mars Silvanus. But it is by no means certain that
Silvanus was originally a cult title of Mars and
Mr. Bailey had made some very pertinent criti-
cisms of this view.

His own suggestion is that Mars was originally
a great *numen* of growth and the growing year,
and that, as such, his worship fell very naturally
to the young warriors of the tribe. He stresses the
analogy between the *Salii* and the Kouretes, the
armed priests of Cretan Zeus, which had attracted
the notice of observers in antiquity, and the
close and striking analogy between their leaping
dances and ritual hymns to which we have already
referred.[1]

We are here in the region of conjecture where
certainty is not to be attained but on the whole
Mr. Bailey's hypothesis seems to be that which

[1] See above, p. 46.

comes nearest to a reasonable solution of the problem without distorting or forcing such fragmentary evidence as we possess.

LECTURE VI

FROM THE ETRUSCAN MONARCHY TO THE PUNIC WARS

In the pages of Livy which narrate the history of the Second Punic War, the topic of religion again and again engages attention. The strain of that prolonged anxiety our generation can but too well appreciate. Hannibal was at large in Italy ; at Trebia, Trasimene and Cannae the armies of the state had been not merely defeated but destroyed. Though disaster followed disaster the undaunted spirit of the Roman people and its leaders did not despair of the commonwealth and maintained the struggle with grim determination. But each year which prolonged it, intensified the mental strain and it was but natural that an anxiety so tortured should turn for relief to the canvassing of religious hopes and fears. The records of each year are marked by the occurrence of prodigies, and a regular procedure inevitably follows their announcement. The Sibylline Books are consulted and upon their recommendation the performance of certain religious rites are officially carried out. Usually these rites consist of *lectisternia*, in which the images of anthropo-morphic gods were exhibited upon couches and were presented with food, or *supplicationes*, in which the population visited the temples in procession and implored divine aid. The contrast of character between these ceremonies and those of the Religion of Numa is complete. What, then is the significance of this change and how is it that it had come about ?

If tradition can be believed the last three kings of Rome were foreigners with Etruscan names. They did much for the material and political development of the community, which they ruled. To the first of them, Servius Tullius Mastarna, was attributed the organisation of the army and the census, and although the so-called Servian wall, of which the ruins are shown at the present day, is a building not older than the sack of Rome by the Gauls in 390 B.C., there is no reason to doubt the soundness of the tradition which ascribes to the Etruscan kings the conversion of Rome into a big fortified city upon the Etruscan model. Stronger alike for offence and defence, the new Rome realised new political ambitions and became the acknowledged leader of the Latin League. The city grew in

size and population no less than in power. Her
favourable position at the crossways of the natural
routes of commerce, which ran up the Tiber
from the outside world into Central Italy and
from Latium to Etruria by the river crossing
guarded by the seven hills, began now to be
exploited. With the foreign tyrants came foreign
merchants and foreign artificers. The new
interests of commerce and handicraft entered the
community.

These secular changes have naturally their
counterpart in the history of Roman religion.
To the Etruscan kings is due the introduction of
temple worship. The simple ritual of the religion
of Numa had been innocent of temples made with
hands. The worship of the early Roman had
taken place at sacred groves ; an altar made of
turf or stone and a small shrine (*sacellum*) were
the most elaborate buildings of which it made use.
The Etruscans, however, whose native civilisation
was in the main a debased Hellenism, introduced
the more splendid housing of their objects of
worship in permanent structures highly orna-
mented by Graeco-Etruscan art. In themselves
these new and magnificent homes assisted the
individualisation of Roman *numina* and fostered
the development of the conception of gods as

divine personalities.   It was natural too that
with the introduction of temples came the
practice of representing their divine inhabitants
by statues.   Art, as indeed it had already shown in
Greece, is a powerful factor in the moulding of
popular conceptions of the nature of divinities
and for obvious reasons in Greece and Rome,
where it rejected the half-human half-bestial
representations of divinity, like those, for example,
known to Egypt, its influence was strongly
anthropomorphic.

Another great change in Roman religion also
begins to manifest itself in the period of the
Etruscan rulers. The new political position of
Rome necessitated the definition of the attitude of
the Roman state towards the deities of conquered
or subordinate communities. To supplement the
deficiencies of the existing state religion which
was purely agricultural in character the Romans
adopted the cults of subject-peoples and of the
foreigners, who were brought in increasing
numbers to trade or to settle in Rome. These
influences caused a great multiplication of the
objects of worship and profoundly altered their
character. For the foreign deities tended either
to be identified with some existing object of
worship, in which case the older conception of the

power in question was modified by the addition of new characteristics or features belonging properly to the foreign deity thus identified with it, or by their greater consonance with the new conditions of society to push the older-fashioned gods into the obscurity of obsoleteness. This was inevitable. For obvious reasons Rome was not to look back nor to become again a primitive agricultural community. All the forces of development were operative in the opposite direction ; her character was bound increasingly to take on the colour of an imperial, commercial and capitalistic society.

These influences which began to be felt under the Etruscan monarchy were operative throughout the period of the early Republic. The changes, which they effected, were promoted by the growing political importance of the Plebeians and their successful struggle for political equality. For while the older religious system remained almost inevitably in Patrician hands, the cults of later introduction, associated with the economic development to which the Plebeians in great measure owed their increased numbers and power, afforded an opportunity for claiming a share in the religious administration of the state.

The Romans divided their gods into two

categories, *di indigetes*, native gods and *di noven-sides* or *novensiles* gods who had settled in Rome. The *di indigites* belong to the religion of Numa. They were members of the oldest community of the four regions and with few exceptions their place of worship lay inside the *pomerium*, the spiritual boundary of the city. Among the new-comers two classes may be distinguished : (1) divinities of Roman creation or introduced from Italian sources, the worship of which was admitted inside the *pomerium* and was conducted under the direct control of the *pontifices* by Roman citizens ; (2) divinities adopted from foreign sources, in this period mainly Greek, the worship of which was not admitted within the *pomerium*, was regulated by a special board of officials distinct from the *pontifices*, and was performed in accordance with their native non-Roman ritual by native priests.

It has been said that the Etruscan kings substituted " a religion of patriotism for a religion of physical increase." The great temple upon the Capitol, first alike in the date of its foundation and in its national importance, was certainly begun, though it may not have been completed, under the Etruscan kings. A triad of divinities, Iupiter, Iuno and Minerva, a combination which corresponded to a divine triad widely worshipped in Eturia, now took the most prominent place in the state religion. Before the rising importance of this triad the three principal figures of the old calendar, Mars, Quirinus and Iupiter fell into the background. In particular Mars, though he never altogether surrendered his claim to be the national patron of the warlike Romans, was supplanted by Iupiter as the god *par excellence* of Rome's political destiny. Iupiter Latiaris was the supreme deity of the Latin League, of which Rome had now become the acknowledged head ; but in the new temple on the Capitol was worshipped a yet more powerful and greater Iupiter than Latiaris or, indeed, than any other, Iupiter Best and Greatest (Optimus Maximus), whose cult is, as it were, the religious expression of Rome's secular aspirations.

The assertion of Rome's political supremacy in the Latin League is also reflected in the introduction of the worship of Diana, whose great temple on the Aventine was founded under the monarchy. Diana was later identified with the Greek Artemis, but originally she was a native Italian goddess who was worshipped by the members of the Latin League in the grove of Aricia. It was this which gave her cult political importance and explains the significance of the transference of its centre of gravity to Rome and to Roman control.

Ancient polytheism was not of course exclusive in the sense of disputing the existence and validity of the gods of other peoples. Rome had therefore to decide her policy towards the divine as well as towards the human inhabitants of the cities which she conquered. There are examples where the divine inhabitants of a beleaguered town were induced to turn traitor to their worshippers. The process was called *evocatio*, and the best known example is the evocation of Iuno Regina, the goddess of Veii. In the course of the siege the Romans made promise in the due religious form that if the goddess would desert the cause of her worshippers for that of the besiegers her cult should be officially established in Rome after the capture of the town.[1]

---

[1] The formula of *evocation* will be found in Macrobius *Sat.*, III, 9, 7. "Si deus, si dea est, cui populus civitasque Carthaginiensis est in tutela, teque maxime, ille qui urbis huius populique tutelam recepisti, precor venerorque veniamque a vobis peto ut vos populum civitatemque Carthaginiensem deseratis, loca templa sacra urbemque eorum relinquatis, absque his abeatis, eique populo civitati metum formidinem oblivionem iniciatis, proditique Romam ad me meosque veniatis nostraque vobis loca templa sacra, urbs acceptior probatiorque sit, mihique populoque Romano militibusque meis propitii sitis, ut sciamus intellegamusque. Si ita feceritis, voveo vobis templa ludosque facturum."

H

In many cases, even where this promise had not been made, the deities of a conquered state were incorporated into the Roman religious system and their cults officially established in Rome. Policy in this matter was of course directed by the *pontifices* and there is no means of knowing for what reason this incorporation was or was not carried out in particular cases. It is certain however that in this way some of the most important cults of the Republican period were first introduced into Rome. For example the worship of Fors Fortuna came thus from Etruria, that of Iuturna from Lavinium, that of Minerva Capta from Falerii, that of Feronia from Capua, and that of Vortumna from Volsinii.

The number of Roman deities therefore tended to increase with the political expansion of Rome ; there was further a tendency towards multiplication by the sub-division of divine concepts. In part no doubt this multiplication is due to the pseudo-scientific pedantry of formalism and the natural tendency of an expert priesthood to elaborate ritual at the expense of common sense. To this tendency must probably be attributed the long lists of *Indigitamenta* which assigned to each minute sub-division of human activity its special and appropriate *numen*. Thus the farmer was called upon to invoke " Vervactorem, Reparatorem, Imporcitorem, Insitorem, Obaratorem, Occatorem, Sarritorem, Subruncinatorem, Messorem, Convectorem, Conditorem and Promitorem," " breaker up of fallow land, renewer, maker of furrows, grafter, plougher, harrower, hoer, weeder, reaper, gatherer, storer, producer." These formulae of invocation are evidently the result of professional elaboration, though they belong quite probably to the later stages of the religion of Numa. They are curious rather than important. Such elaboration must defeat its own ends and strictly speaking, as Wissowa has remarked, it is not so much a creation of new gods which it implies as the ideal dissection of the operation of the divine power. More important is the tendency of cult titles, which denote some special activity or aspect of a deity, to become detached and independent thus creating new objects of worship. In itself the process is a natural one of which many examples could be given from the history of Greek religion. In Roman religion it was an important factor in the multiplication of deities and to it must be attributed the deification of many abstractions. Thus the divinities Fides and Libertas have their origin in cult titles of Iupiter ; Honos and Virtus, the military qualities *par excellence*, were attributes of Mars before they received the honour of independent deification. The deification of abstractions came peculiarly easily to a people of the Latin stock whose native religious system was rooted in numinism and whose early formulae might contain such phrases as that considered on p. 94 above.

Abstract divinities like Concordia, Spes or Pietas, the origin of which cannot be traced in the cult titles of earlier deities, may perhaps be accounted for as deifications prompted by the analogy of Honos and Virtus and the like.

Thus far we have been considering new cults which were either introduced by the Etruscan kings, created by Roman religious authorities, or incorporated with the political incorporation of their native places in the Roman state. There remain the deities, whose worship came to Rome with the new population of what had become a civilised centre of an active commercial and urban life. Thus Minerva, the goddess of handicraft, came first from Southern Etruria, probably from Falerii, with the Etruscan workmen who flocked to Rome under the later monarchy.

Capitol, but the control of their consultation was vested in the Senate, who alone could authorise their use on behalf of the state. Indeed the existence of a body of prophecy under official control was characteristically turned to account. The public circulation of unauthorised prophecies, a potential source of popular emotional and religious disorder, became illegal and popular prophecies received an honourable extinction in being removed from circulation for incorporation in the state collection.

The Sibylline Books were consulted upon occasions when the community suffered from some misfortune, which appeared to indicate that the wrath of heaven had been incurred. The remedies to avert divine displeasure, which they recommended, were invariably the celebration of religious rites in honour of some god or goddess, who in fact was usually Greek. In this way the books of prophecy became the most powerful agent in the introduction of Greek cults into Roman religion.

The prophetic powers of the Sibyl were derivative and it can hardly be doubted that the worship of Apollo, the source of her inspiration, reached Rome as early as the Books of Prophecy. According to tradition the same

Tarquin, who bought them from the mysterious crone, sent a deputation to Greece to consult the oracle of Apollo at Delphi. The first temple of Apollo, however, was vowed in 433 B.C., in accordance with the advice of the Sibylline Books which had been consulted in consequence of a severe pestilence and was not completed until 431 B.C.

In 496 B.C. the harvest failed and under the stress of famine the Books were consulted. The Romans were recommended to introduce the worship of the Greek divinities Demeter, Dionysos and Kore who were to be identified with the Italian Ceres, Liber and Libera respectively. The temple consequently vowed was completed in 493 B.C. by Greek artists, Damophilus and Gorgasus. In similar moments of emergency the adoption of other Greek cults was ordered. Thus, for example, Hermes Empolaios entered Rome under the Latin name of Mercurius and Poseidon was identified with Neptunus.

The Greeks gods so introduced assumed in many cases a Latin name but they retained both their native rites and the stories which attached to them in their Greek form. These identifications therefore imply the introduction of foreign elements in two most important spheres of religion, ritual and mythology. In 399 B.C. a winter of great severity had been followed by a hot season and plague. *Religio*, in its primary sense of religious apprehension, was naturally aroused to seek the means of averting divine wrath by the forms of religious ceremonial. The Sibylline Books were consulted and for the first time the Greek rite of a *lectisternium* was celebrated in Rome. A festival of eight days was proclaimed during which the effigies of three pairs of deities, Apollo and Latona, Diana and Hercules, Mercurius and Neptunus were publicly exposed upon couches with tables containing offerings of food before them.

It will be noticed that the deities concerned in this ceremonial are without exception Greek though some have acquired by identification Latin names. The ritual is Greek. The completely anthropomorphic character of the ideas expressed in presenting a banquet to divine beings is absolutely foreign to the numinism of early Rome. The popular and spectacular character of the rite may also be emphasised. This is even more prominent in the ritual of *supplicationes*, which were now introduced under Sibylline influence, to provide religious help in time of trouble. When a *supplicatio* was proclaimed, the whole people, men, women and children marched in processions to the temples carrying the sacred laurel branches of Greek piacular ritual and prostrated themselves before the images of the gods to implore divine assistance. The old Latin idea that religious duty consisted in the meticulously accurate performance of ritual by official experts while the part played by the laity is confined to abstention from any action likely to obstruct or negative the result, has disappeared. The whole people takes part in these emotional ceremonies and finds in their performance a real distraction and emotional satisfaction in times of great trouble. In fact with the growing complexity of civilised life the emotional needs of the individual for religious expression and satisfaction became increasingly urgent and this factor played no small part in the supersession of the old Latin formalism by the new and more imaginative Greek ritual as it did again later in the propagation of the still more personal and emotional cults of the East.

The political expansion of Rome naturally intensified the influence of Greek ideas in all departments of life. The conquest of the Greek towns of South Italy was followed by the First Punic War, the war for Sicily. From this direct

contact Roman literature was born in the trans-
lations of Greek originals by the Greek captive,
who became the first Roman poet and dramatist,
and the spoils of Greek towns introduced Hellenic
art to Rome. The acid of Greek philosophy
eventually permeated the intelligentsia, to the
destruction of faith and the disintegration of
Roman discipline and institutions, but of that
period the two great Scipios and their circles
mark only the beginning. The Second Punic War
defines the limit of an earlier stage in which Greek
cult has been virtually substituted for Roman and
the new deities have so far ousted the old that the
distinction between old and new gods is practically
lost, but faith has not yet been destroyed by
Greek philosophy and in the great need of a
national crisis recourse is had to divine assistance.

The long lists of prodigies in Livy reflect the
acuteness of the strain of the Hannibalic invasion
upon the people's nerves. The situation was
skilfully handled by the religious officials. In
part no doubt their hopes of effectively obtaining
divine aid by the measures, which they prescribed,
were perfectly genuine but at the same time we
may notice how admirably the ceremonies served
by their spectacular character to distract and calm
the popular emotion. In 218 B.C. after the report

of alarming prodigies the Sibylline Books were consulted and a *lectisternium* and *supplicationes* were held. In 217 B.C. the disaster of Trasimene was followed by further prodigies. *Ludi,* sacred games on the Greek model, were held and a *lectisternium* on a grand scale took place, twelve deities being feasted in pairs. In this year too was revived an old Latin ritual by which a community in desperate straits might win divine assistance. The sacred spring (*ver sacrum*) was proclaimed which meant that all the produce, including the children, of the spring five years after the date of the ceremony, were to be dedicated to the god, if the state proved then to have survived the crisis. In the old Latin rite such vows of dedication were made to Mars but Iupiter had now become the national god of Rome and upon this occasion it was to the god of the Capitoline temple that the vow was made.

In 216 B.C. after Cannae the occurrence of alleged scandals in connection with the Vestal Virgins as well as the announcement of prodigies testify to the acuteness of popular anxiety. Fabius Pictor, the father of Roman history, was sent on a mission to the god of Delphi and the exceptional strain of the time is reflected in the burying alive of a pair of Gauls and a pair of

Greeks, for human sacrifice was quite foreign to
Roman religion in normal times. In 213 B.C. we
find the authorities taking in hand the religious
excitement, which the protracted strain of war had
produced particularly, it is interesting to notice,
among the women of Rome. Private superstitions
were rigidly suppressed and a distraction to keep
the people quiet and to provide an innocuous outlet for religious feeling was provided by the foundation of the Games of Apollo, *Ludi Apollinares*,
a festival of course upon the Greek model. In
205 B.C. when Scipio was appointed for the final
and decisive effort of invading Africa, the cult of
the Great Mother of Asia Minor was brought to
Rome. The black stone which represented her
presence was officially welcomed by Scipio, as
representative of the State and for the first time
one of the orgiastic cults of the East gained an
official footing in Rome.

The end of the Second Punic War closes an
epoch not only in the history of Rome but also in
the history of Roman religion. During the period
which had elapsed since the monarchy Greek gods
and Greek mythology had invaded Rome. Foreign
rites had largely superseded the older religion of
the state and the process had gone so far that the
distinction between the old gods and the new was

I

practically lost. But this worship of Graeco-Roman deities had still a real importance for national consciousness and proved a real help throughout the Hannibalic War. At the same time the religious instrument was to some extent deliberately handled by the authorities for secular purposes. Their skill was shown in the way in which they steadied popular apprehension and, while suppressing hysteria of any kind, provided a sufficient outlet for religious feeling.

LECTURE VII

In the sixth ode of his third book Horace addresses his fellow countrymen. He looks back from the dawn of the Augustan age over a century of discord, faction and civil war and gives his diagnosis of the causes of the miseries of the time. It lies, he thinks, in the decay of religion and morals. The new generation of Romans will continue to pay the penalty in public and private misfortune until the sins of their fathers are abjured. The temples which have fallen into decay must be rebuilt and religious discipline restored. The Parthians had easily triumphed over armies which despised the taking of the auspices. Irreligion and luxury had sapped private morals and old fashioned family discipline had disappeared. Young women begin with a craze for indecorous foreign dances (*Ionicos motus*) and end with adultery and the murder of their husbands. These are not the morals which made Rome great. They were the simple virtues of a rustic peasantry, hard working, disciplined and brought up from early youth to

131

show a proper reverence for their parents and the gods. The text of the sermon is that of the new regime, which Augustus was trying to create. It is of course a sermon and preached upon a familiar rhetorical contrast between the virtuous peasant and the idle, vicious, and urban rich. Nevertheless there is a good deal in its accusations and they will perhaps repay our attention.

The misery of the last hundred years of the Republic is indisputable. It is a century of revolutions, civil wars and proscriptions, a period of complete anarchy when neither life nor property were secure. We are perhaps a little prone to regard the events of these years of violence as a highly coloured spectacle exciting our emotional interest only by the rapidity and violence of its vicissitudes and to forget the conditions of life which these political events imply for the individuals who were so unfortunate as to be their contemporaries. The peculiar horror of the time, as it has been well said, was that it put the better elements of society at the mercy of the worse. The fourth book of Appian's history of the Civil Wars or even the implications of the *Laudatio Turiae* will give a vivid impression of what it must have been like to be an ordinary decent Roman in the days of the proscriptions, with unmerited exile or sudden death an ever present menace, and the possibility of your nearest relation or most trusted servant revealing himself without warning as an enemy and an executioner.[1]

The Second Punic War had been followed by Rome's conquest of the East. Her spoils had concentrated in her hands the capital of the Mediterranean world and her conquests had flooded the market with slaves. Luxury and materialism characterised the upper classes and the extended scale of slavery brought with it its attendant evils. The plantation gangs filled Italy with a potential source of armed disorder and the free Romans of the lower classes degenerated into an urban rabble of " mean whites." Roman institutions, devised as they had been for a city state, failed to meet the demands of administering an empire. In politics a jealous and decadent aristocracy struggled to maintain its monopoly of political privilege against the claims advanced by the newly arisen capitalists or by the leaders, who succeeded in organising the violence of the worthless mob to further their own political ambitions. The central government, whatever politicians might be in control, was powerless to assert its

[1] A translation of Appian's *Civil Wars* will be found in Appian's *Roman History* (Loeb Classical Library), Vol. IV. For the *Laudatio Turiæ* see Warde Fowler, *Social Life in the Age of Cicero*, pp. 159 f.

authority over the commanders of professional
armies, with whom it could not dispense. Individualism was the note of the age. Sulla's
veterans called themselves *Sullani*, the men of
Sulla, not soldiers of the state. Force had been
revealed as the sole basis of authority first in the
guise of mob violence and later in the yet more
vicious form of military dictatorship.

Periods of anarchy and insecurity such as these,
are likely to be marked by a cynical disregard of
all moral laws and by the substitution of a combination of scepticism and superstition for the
discarded sanctions of religion. The institutions
of the state and the old discipline of family life
alike broke down. The moral and religious decay
of the period is at once a symptom and a sub-
sidiary cause of its miseries.

We have seen that right up to the end of the
Second Punic War religion was still a real force
in the life of the state. It was a religion much
altered, it is true, from the religion of Numa.
Greek mythology had changed the character of
the old Latin objects of worship, the most
frequent state ceremonies consisted of *lectisternia*
and *supplicationes*, rites which were foreign not
Roman in origin; the distinction between *di
indigetes* and *di novensiles* had become academic

only. But none the less religion was still a powerful motive force in men's lives and in serious crises the state turned to religion for help. If however we turn our attention to the times in which Cicero or his father lived, we shall find a very different attitude of mind displayed both in the manipulation of the forms of the state religion for political purposes and in the religious beliefs of individuals.

With regard to the state religion Horace has already told us that the temples from neglect were falling into decay. From 89—11 B.C., the oldest and most important officiating priesthood, that of *Flamen Dialis*, remained vacant. The reason was simply that no one could be found to fill a priesthood which conferred no political power and the holder of which was debarred from secular office. There was no difficulty of course in filling places on the boards of *augures* or *pontifices ;* Cicero was an augur and Caesar pontifex maximus. Such offices were not only dignified in themselves but they in no way interfered with the simultaneous holding of secular office and even conferred an authority in religious matters which might prove useful in an age when the forms of religion were cynically used as instruments of political warfare.

For example in 59 B.C. Caesar was bringing in

his agrarian law in the teeth of senatorial opposition. He appealed to the people and disregarded the veto of a tribune, who was put up to obstruct the passage of the bill. His fellow consul, Bibulus, proving intractable, was driven away by Pompey's soldiers and as a last resort fell back upon a religious weapon. Every day he gave notice of " watching the heavens " and thereby in accordance with technical religious law put a stop to all public business. Caesar, who was not only consul but also pontifex maximus, simply ignored the obstruction. The whole incident shows to what a pass the state religion had come and how little real meaning its forms still possessed.

The calendar provides another illustration. When Caesar took it in hand it was more than two months out of the true reckoning. How had this come about ? Originally the publication of the calendar had been an important duty of the religious authorities as part of the *ius divinum*. From the beginning the *pontifices* had found a difficulty in adjusting the lunar to the solar year though such adjustment was very necessary to the farmer if his agricultural festivals were to keep in harmony with the seasons. In 450 B.C. a Greek system working on a cycle of four years had been adopted ; the first and third years contained

355 days, to the second and fourth 22 and 23 days were added respectively. This gave an excess of four days every four years and to adjust the discrepancy the *pontifices* had power to make intercalation when necessary.

In the first century B.C. however the *pontifices* used this power less to remedy defects in the calendar than to promote political purposes of the moment, to prolong a command or to delay a date. For example, in 50 B.C. the question of intercalation came up. Cicero was anxious that it should be prevented for it would mean for him another month of exile in his provincial governorship; Curio, on the other hand, was agitating for it in order to prolong his own term of office and to postpone the date of Caesar's surrender of his province.[1]

The regulation of the calendar, which was in essence a religious duty and an important part of *ius divinum*, had in fact become a mere instrument for political wire-pulling.

These examples may illustrate how the forms of the state religion were cynically exploited for political purposes and their abuse was pushed to the extreme of making religious ordinances

[1] Cicero, *ad Fam.*, viii, 6; a translation will be found in Jeans, *Life and Letters of Cicero*, No. 35.

ridiculous. Clearly there is little vitality or genuine religious feeling left in a system so treated.

The attitude of individuals no less betrays the fact that the old sanctions of religion have dissolved. Lucretius cannot, perhaps, be called an irreligious person. His attack upon religion has itself a genuinely religious fervour and he is a true prophet, although his message to the world is salvation by scientific rationalism. Science in the poet's view is the only true guide ; religion is based upon a series of fictions which human folly has invented and from this superstition ultimately derive all human ills. Lucretius is of course a great poet and a great thinker but genius, although it cannot fairly be regarded as representative of its ordinary contemporaries, is not wholly independent of its environment. The attack of Lucretius at least shows that irreligion was in the air and that the forms of Roman worship were not fulfilling the spiritual needs of the time.

The contemporary of Lucretius, who dominated the political stage, was Lucius Cornelius Sulla, politically a reactionary doctrinaire who was enabled, thanks to the army at his back, to force his constitutional panacea upon his countrymen. In the attainment of his end he was completely ruthless and indifferent as to the means which he employed. The system which he originated of cold-blooded murder by proscription shows us a man undeterred by any moral or sentimental scruple. He too is a product of his time, what is his attitude towards religion ?

Plutarch's *Life*, which is founded in part upon the memoirs of the man himself, portrays a character not uncommon in an age when received systems of religion have broken down. It is a mixture of scepticism and superstition. On the one hand there is a contempt for religious institutions and a lack of reverence for religious laws. In his Greek campaign Sulla did not hesitate to cut down sacred groves in order to obtain material for the construction of his siege engines. He stole the temple treasures of Epidaurus and Olympia and at Delphi he did not shrink from adding blasphemous insult to injury. To the protest of the Amphictyons he answered that he would keep the treasure more safely than the god and when it was alleged that the sound of a harp had been heard to issue miraculously from the inner shrine while his envoys were removing the gold he " replied in a scoffing way that it was surprising to him that Caphis did not know that music was a sign of joy not anger ; he should therefore go on boldly and accept what a gracious and bountiful god offered." The same man was intensely superstitious. He believed like Napoleon in his star; he adopted the name of Fortunate (*Felix*) and called his children by names of good omen, *Faustus* and *Fausta*. He felt the attraction of the strange and emotional cult of the Cappadocian goddess, which appealed to him, in much the same way that spiritualism or some Oriental esoteric faith appears in our own day to attract many who are sceptical about the dogmas of Christianity. He attached great weight to ominous occurrences and invariably carried about with him a small golden figure of Apollo.

No doubt none of us is continuously consistent in his religious belief and practice but here the inconsistency is acute. It is marked also in the attitude of Cicero towards religious matters. Cicero was not only an augur but proud of his tenure of that dignity. His pride, however, rests rather upon his natural conservatism and his respect for established institutions than upon religious conviction. As regards the forms of state religion Cicero, as a statesman and a constitutionalist, is keenly alive to their political value. He is a buttress of the established church. But Cicero the philosopher is hampered by no religious bias nor convictions. He debates in a perfectly free way the question whether augury has any validity and his book on divination reaches a sceptical conclusion. Cicero, the public man, believed in an established religion as a useful element in the constitution ; Cicero, the philosopher in his study, had a completely open mind.

Of course no human being is consistently either a philosopher or a statesman. An interesting trio happened to be together at Dyrrachium awaiting the report of a decisive battle between Caesar and Pompey, Varro, the great antiquarian, Cato and Cicero. The rumour of a prophecy by a Rhodian sailor that Greece would be drenched with blood filled these three philosophers with a terrified foreboding, which shortly afterwards was justified by the arrival of the news of Pharsalia.

In moments too of real emotion the man is carried beyond his agnosticism or scepticism. The phenomenon is not unusual and there are many who are ready, like the Melians in Thucydides,[1] to turn to religion when other helpers flee. Warde Fowler has well brought out the effect upon Cicero of his beloved daughter's death. For Cicero, the student, the immortality of the soul is a matter for philosophic debate but

[1] Thucydides, V, 143.

when Tullia dies the bereaved father builds for her not a tomb (*sepulchrum*) but a shrine (*fanum*). " I wish to have a shrine built," he tells his friend " and that wish cannot be rooted out of my heart. I am anxious to avoid any likeness to a tomb, not so much on account of the penalty of the law as in order to attain as nearly as possible to apotheosis."[1]

Cicero's normal attitude towards religion is displayed in the treatise *On the Nature of Gods*, where he early lays it down that the existence of Gods is necessary to maintain the ordered fabric of the social system and to sanction the virtues which hold society together.[2] In a well-known speech he declares that religious feeling is a characteristic national Roman trait. " In piety and in religion and in this one science by which we have perceived that all things are ruled and governed by the will of the immortal gods, we have surpassed all races and nations."[3] To this quality Livy through the mouth of Camillus attributes the source of Rome's success. " Examine the good and bad fortunes of these years in order ; you will find that when we followed the gods

---

[1] *ad Att.*, XII, 12, 1, and XII, 36, 1.

[2] Cicero, *de Natura Deorum*, 1, 2. 3.

[3] Cicero, *de Har. Resp.*, 9.

everything turned out well, when we neglected them everything went ill with us."[1]

Polybius, the wise and observant admirer of the expansion of Roman power, who was the personal friend of Scipio the Younger, expresses much the same sentiments. His explanation of the phenomenon further gives the clue to one of the principal causes of its decay. "The most remarkable difference for the better between the Roman and Carthaginian states is in religious matters. Indeed it seems to me that what is regarded as a weakness by other men has held together the fortunes of Rome, I mean the fear of spiritual powers." (Deisidaimonia, the word thus literally translated, had a derogatory bias and is almost equivalent to superstition.) "For the rôle which it plays both in their private life and their public affairs can hardly be exaggerated. This will seem surprising to many. I believe myself that this has been brought about for the sake of the proletariat. In a state composed of wise men, if such were possible, perhaps such an attitude would not be necessary but since every crowd is unstable and full of unlimited desires and unreasoning anger and violent passion it remains to control it by unseen fears and similar poetic fictions."[2]

[1] Livy, V, 51.   [2] Polybius, VI, 56.

With this passage may be compared the dictum
of Quintus Mucius Scaevola which St. Augustine
has naturally turned to good account.[1] When
Cicero was a young man, Scaevola was perhaps
the most revered figure in Rome. He was not
only *Pontifex Maximus*, but he was reputed to be
the most learned and the greatest of those who
had held the office. This official head of Roman
religion laid it down that religion may be divided
into three kinds : (1) the fictions of the poets,
which are ornamental merely ; (2) the religion of
philosophy ; (3) the religion of the state which
exists to assist the statesman in the management
of the lower orders.

The religion of Cicero's age, as Warde Fowler
has pointed out, had in fact become completely
divorced from life and it is clear that when its
ritual has come to be openly regarded by its
official representatives as consisting of mere
forms to be maintained for the benefit of the
proletariat or to be manipulated for the purposes
of statecraft, it has ceased to be a spiritual factor in
the nation's life. For no religion can continue
to exist as a living force when belief in its essential
truth is dead or moribund.

The causes, which had brought Roman religion

---

[1] Augustine, *de Civ. Dei*, IV, 27.

to this pass, though complex are not unintelligible. We have already noticed that the religion of Numa betrays the legal bias of the national temperament in an exaggerated emphasis upon the importance of correct procedure. The relation of the individual or the state towards spiritual powers has almost a contractual character. Any error, however slight and irrespective of its motive, was held to invalidate the proceedings. Religious ritual was therefore left in the hands of experts ; formalism was carried to its logical extreme ; the religious authorities, like dexterous lawyers, found an escape from difficulties in the manipulation of regulations. The letter of the law became more important than the spirit.

Two well-known examples may bear repetition. In the Second Punic War Marcellus, when in command, was carried about in a litter with the blinds drawn in order to prevent the possibility of his seeing anything of ill omen. In 293 B.C. the keeper of the sacred chickens, from the behaviour of which in feeding omens were drawn, falsely reported the omens good. The commander on hearing of this ruled that, whatever might have happened in fact, the omens had been officially reported as good and therefore were good,

K

though he punished the chicken keeper by putting him in the front line of battle.

Even the ordinary practice with regard to the sacred chickens, as Cicero remarked,[1] is not devoid of disingenuousness. It was a good omen if the birds fell so greedily upon their food that some grains dropped from their mouths. It was the rule to secure this desirable assurance by keeping the chickens for days beforehand closely cooped and without food. Such artificiality is ultimately at variance with commonsense. The development of formalism thus did much to kill reverence for religion by making it unreal and even ridiculous.

The view that religion supplies an instrument to the statesman may be traced back to the period of the Second Punic War. We have already noticed the wise direction of religious ceremonies by the authorities. Religious fears were allayed by the introduction of foreign rites, which in themselves provided a means of popular distraction, and at the same time emotionalism and hysteria were put down with a firm hand. A more conscious employment of religion for purposes of political expediency follows the conclusion of the war with Hannibal. It was necessary in the interests of

[1] Cicero, *De div.*, II, 34.

Rome to take up the challenge of the Eastern powers but to induce the citizens to embark upon a new foreign war was not easy. Besides concessions as regards military service and the circulation of rumours of a projected invasion of Italy by Macedon, the religious machinery was set in motion to reconcile the proletariat to an unpopular but necessary policy. From this it is but a short step to the use of similar means in the narrower interests of party or of political intrigue. In 199 B.C. the friends of the commander whom he was to supersede, secured the report of prodigies to prevent Flamininus from taking up his duties in Macedonia. Henceforward religious regulations were freely used for obstruction in political warfare. The result was naturally to discredit their validity. We have seen Caesar ignoring the watching of the heavens by Bibulus and Crassus, though less fortunate in the event, over-rode the religious obstacles raised by his political opponents to prevent his departure for the Parthian expedition.

A cynical abuse of religion of a different kind but equally illustrative of the temper of the age was the appointment in 209 B.C. of the black sheep of a distinguished family, C. Valerius Flaccus, to the office of *rex sacrorum*. His relatives procured his nomination because it was hoped that the innumerable taboos with which this ancient office was hedged would inevitably keep the young man straight.

Religion, then, in the third aspect given in Scaevola's analysis, had become by the first century, B.C. mere empty ceremonial destitute of real meaning. The politicians, who cynically manipulated its rules, had no religious convictions and their dupes were hardly deceived by artifice so patent. The masses, it is true, are always liable to waves of religious emotion or superstition, but it remains impossible "to fool all the people all the time" and a religion, which is regarded by its leaders as a mere instrument of statecraft, is too devoid of sincerity long to deceive the masses.

The religion described as consisting of the mere ornamental fictions of the poets had no roots in the national temperament. Mythology was a foreign accretion and so far from being an organic part of Roman religion it was in reality inconsistent with the religious ideas which numinism represents. Anthropomorphism has its obvious moral weaknesses and it is perhaps even true to say that there are greater possibilities of religious development in the worship of unpersonified spiritual powers than in that of clear cut anthro-

pomorphic deities whose idealised figures may
have a more than human beauty but must retain
the frailties associated with human personality.

It must be remembered further that at the
date when Greek influences became dominant in
Rome, Greek religion had passed its prime. The
Greeks themselves had ceased to take their
mythology seriously. Its immoral stories, which
philosophers rejected as false or attempted to
explain away, afforded topics for jest upon the
comic stage. But Roman literature was derivative
from Greek and in particular Roman comedy
took, not merely its inspiration but even its
form and subject matter directly from the New
Greek Comedy in which this humorous treatment of mythological topics was a favourite
feature. The influence of the comic stage upon
the Roman lower classes was not less potent
than the influence of Greek philosophy upon
the upper. It was inevitable that the habitual
spectacle of the representation of gods in
ludicrous, undignified and unseemly situations
should undermine reverence and sincerity of
religious belief. The plot of Plautus' *Amphitryon*
will sufficiently illustrate the destructive influence
which Comedy thus brought to bear. " Iupiter,
being seized with love for Alcmena, changed his

form to that of her husband, Amphitryon, while he was doing battle with his enemies in defence of his country. Mercury, in the guise of Sosia seconds his father and dupes both master and servant on their return. Amphitryon storms at his wife ; charges of adultery too are bandied back and forth between him and Iupiter. Blepharo is appointed arbiter but is unable to decide which is the real Amphitryon. They learn the whole truth at last and Alcmena gives birth to twin sons."

The changed social conditions of the urban poor worked powerfully in the same direction to undermine belief in the old religion. This had been rooted in the family life of the peasant farmer with its distinctive discipline, corporate sense and civic virtues. Where in rural Italy the peasant farmer survived, the old rites, which were the religious expression of this simple life, were still observed. But the poor in the Roman capital could no longer be said to possess a family life. Capitalism and slavery had produced an urban proletariat miserably poor but too proud to work at servile occupations. For the environment of family life in the small homestead was substituted existence in a corner of some crowded tenement and at death the pauper's body was cast into a common burial pit. At the other end of the social scale the old family life had equally disappeared though for opposite reasons. In the gigantic households and ostentatious palaces and villas of the millionaire it could hardly be expected to survive. Both the careless luxury of the rich and the desperate misery of the poor produced a tendency towards materialism and indifference to spiritual issues.

The disappearance of family discipline and the sense of family unity both at the top and at the bottom of the social scale abetted the growth of individualism which was an inevitable product of the development of a more complex civilisation. In the upper classes the emancipation of women was a feature of the age, the attendant extravagances of which were accentuated by the suddenness of its accomplishment. This growth of individualism is reflected in the sepulchral inscriptions. For the first time in the first century B.C. a belief in personal immortality is implied by reference to the Manes of an individual[1] and the *Laudatio Turiae* concludes " I pray that thy divine Manes (*di Manes tui*) may keep thee in peace and watch over thee."

Religion was now called upon to satisfy more

[1] C.I.L. I., 639.

personal and emotional needs. In times of wide-spread temporal anxiety and distress the appeal of the promise of a better life than this becomes irresistible. The very poor are attracted by hopes of a world in which the injustices of this existence will be rectified by divine readjustment. Side by side with cynical materialism there developed in consequence a sense of anxiety about the soul and an absorbing interest in the prospects of a future life. Neither the old Roman religion nor the imported but state-controlled cults were fitted to satisfy this longing. The Pythagorean Orphic societies, whose native home was in Magna Graecia, in part supplied the need though they remained unauthorised and private associations which indeed the state had upon an occasion to suppress as subversive of decency and public morals. But still more effective was the appeal of the various emotional cults of the East which from this period onwards increasingly gained adherents in Roman society. It is not surprising that their earliest proselytes were chiefly drawn from the lower orders or from the ranks of the newly emancipated women. " You followed the religious rites of your family and your state and admitted no foreign cults or degraded magic," records her husband amongst the peculiar excellences of Turia. It will be observed as characteristic that in the third poem of the first book of Tibullus, Delia turns naturally to the Egyptian goddess Isis, the poet to the old Roman family gods. " Now aid me, goddess, now—that thou canst heal saith a crowd of painted panels in thy temples—that my Delia may pay the nightly vigils of her vow, sitting all swathed in linen before thy holy door and twice in the day be bound to chant thy praise with loosened tresses for all to mark amid the Pharian throng. And be it mine many times to stand before the shrine of my sires' Penates and offer incense, as the months come round, to the old Lar of my home."[1]

It remains to say something of the religion of philosophy. To attempt adequately to summarise the content of the systems of philosophy, which Rome learned from the Greeks, would demand more space than is at our disposal but the main directions in which they influenced the Roman attitude towards religion must briefly be noted. For among the upper classes, the intellectual aristocracy, philosophy had become the successful rival of religion. Now the temper of Greek philosophy was directly contrary to that un-

---

[1] Tibullus, I, iii, 27-32 (trans. Postgate, *Loeb Classical Library*).

reasoning respect for authority and tradition which had been characteristic of the early Romans. It introduced the spirit of speculation and questioning. It was essentially analytical and acted as a solvent upon institutions which had been built up upon a basis of unreasoning obedience to custom and precedent. In Greece itself, while maintaining an outward respect for the forms of civic religion, it had attempted to find a rational, in place of a religious sanction for conduct. In particular it had rejected the immoralities of mythology as falsehoods inconsistent with the goodness of god and explained away stories, which appeared too childish to earn the credence of the wise man, as allegorical not literal truths.

At the beginning of the third century B.C., Euhemerus had suggested a rationalistic explanation of the origin of mythology. The stories of the gods were in his view distorted history. Great and good kings of early times had been deified by the grateful recollection of subsequent generations and the Greek gods were in fact human benefactors of mankind, who had undergone apotheosis. This view, that gods were not merely anthropomorphic but had been actually human beings, clearly cuts at the roots of religious belief. It gained considerable acceptance at Rome

and Ennius, the great national poet of the Second
Punic War, published a translation of Euhemerus'
work.

Of the Greek philosophical systems two are
of the first importance in their influence upon
Roman thought, Epicureanism and Stoicism.
Of these the first openly avowed agnosticism.
Epicurus, the son of an Athenian schoolmaster
living in Samos, was born about the middle of the
fourth century B.C. Although he did not dog-
matically deny the existence of gods he asserted
the impossibility of any knowledge as to their
nature or of establishing any contact with them.
If they existed they were too remote to be
interested in man. The universe he believed to
be moved not by a divine but by a mechanical
power and in conduct he preached a form of
quietism. The wise man will pursue enlightened
self interest and that lies in the suppression of
needs, for though thus hedonistic in principle, the
philosophy of Epicurus did not regard gross
pleasures but rather the reduction of wants or
desires as the good. Although theoretically
agnostic Epicureanism was in practice sceptical.
Epicurus himself approved of performing cus-
tomary religious duties on the ground that they
made no difference. Some of his followers how-

ever attacked established religion. Whether god existed or not in complete remoteness from human affairs, the gods of received religion were fictions which must be exposed; for the delusive superstition, which men call religious belief, is the source of fears and angers and passions which are destructive of the good life. That is the theme of Lucretius, the greatest after Virgil of the Roman poets.

The philosophical system however which was most consonant with Roman character, which was interested primarily in conduct rather than speculation, was Stoicism. This school, which blended Oriental elements with Greek, had been founded at Athens by Zeno (345—265 B.C.), a Semite from Cyprus. Its doctrines were introduced to the Roman world by Panaetius, a close friend, like Polybius, of the younger Scipio, whose work was continued in the following century by Posidonius of Rhodes, who, like Zeno, was of Semitic origin and was born at Apamea in Syria. The Stoics believed in the existence of God whom they identified with Reason and supported their conviction by the argument from design. In their view an ordered universe presupposed the existence of a controlling intelligence just as in less perfectly regular human affairs, the existence of order and method in a house, gymnasium or forum necessarily implies that some controlling intelligence has laid down rules. This Reason or God pervades the whole universe and can be understood as Ceres on land, Neptune on the sea and so on. This view that gods of polytheism are aspects of the Divine Reason reconciles philosophy with the religious practice of the ordinary man. At the same time it will be noticed that its tendency is strongly in the direction of monotheism.

The ethical position of the Stoics is determined by the view that what distinguishes man from the lower animals is the possession of reason. This is the higher and better part of his nature and enlightened self-interest will recommend the fullest possible realisation of his better and more rational self. Stoicism therefore preaches social duty and self-respect but differs markedly from Christianity in leaving no room for the idea of self-sacrifice.

From the position taken up by the Stoics that Reason was the sole reality it followed that the accidents of existence are unreal and will be ignored by the Wise Man. Thus by a different route the Wise Man is led round again to an indifference to the chances of existence and to a form of fatalism.

Stoicism is severely intellectual in tone and its ideal is the Wise Man. To women it offers no place; but feminine needs, as we have seen, were supplied from a different source, the emotional religions of the East. Its teaching may be cold and exacting but of its practical value there can be little question. It did supply an austere standard of noble conduct and with its emphasis upon courage and self-respect it appealed to what was best in Roman character.

We have seen that in this period emotional and individual aspirations and needs make themselves felt, which tended to find satisfaction in foreign religions which held out promise of immortality in a better world. They also affected philosophy and Neo-Pythagorean and Platonic doctrines were grafted on to Stoicism. The home of Pythagoreanism had been in Southern Italy; its speculations had been much concerned with the question of immortality of which the solution it suggested was the transmigration of souls or a chain of incarnations leading up to apotheosis. Pythagoreanism was revived by Q. Sextius in the first century B.C. and the Neo-Pythagoreans as they were called laid great stress upon the control of passions and the attainment of purity as a means of cultivating the spiritual and real part of man. Platonism too laid stress upon the distinction between body and soul, the material and the spiritual, and in its later developments had become increasingly mystical. The point of contact between these more mystical systems and Stoicism was found in the Stoic doctrines that God is Reason and that man is distinguished by possessing Reason. The rational element in man was therefore divine and a part of God. As such it was indestructible and immortal. A philosophical basis was thus provided for the hope of apotheosis.

The philosophical doctrines thus too briefly summarised are of immediate interest to our theme because they provided for the upper and intellectual classes what was in fact a substitute for religion. They tolerated in some cases or approved in others the performance of the normal religious observances as social duties or as allegorical representations which though believed literally by the vulgar, conveyed a philosophical truth to which the Wise Man possessed the key. Religion, however, which is explained away as something else, has lost the objective sincerity upon which it depends for vitality.

LECTURE VIII

THE AUGUSTAN REVIVAL

In the last chapter we have considered the decay
of Roman religion and have analysed some of its
causes. In 31 B.C. it apparently had ceased to
exist in any real sense. Why then did Augustus
attempt to revive it ? The character of that
great man remains an enigma but we shall
probably be safe in rejecting any attribution of
prophetic fervour or burning religious conviction
to the great founder of the Empire. So far as
can be judged Augustus would seem personally
to have been at once cynical and superstitious,
certainly not a character with a strong religious
sense such as Virgil perhaps may have been.
We must look more probably for political motives
and in religious policy, as elsewhere, we may
admire the astonishing dexterity, the long views
and the almost uncannily skilful adaptation of
means to his end which characterised Augustus'
work.

The political mission of Augustus was to carry
out successfully the ideas of Iulius Caesar by

avoiding his mistakes in method. He was called upon to put an end to anarchy and civil war by establishing the strong central authority of an autocrat. This however could only be carried through with safety and with any prospect of permanence by the representation that he had restored the republic. His real autocracy was hidden by a screen of make-believe and his constitution was one gigantic fiction. The fiction was necessary but it involved inevitable penalties and Augustus was naturally anxious to make use of any indirect means of supporting the permanence of a magistracy, which in constitutional theory did not exist. For this purpose religion supplied a most effective instrument. The name Augustus itself, the meaning of which is equivalent to " by the Grace of God," with its implications of Divine Right, was assumed in accordance with this policy.

A policy of religious reform had indeed many political advantages to recommend it. Aristotle has remarked of the Greek tyrant, who upon a smaller stage performed a task not dissimilar to that of Augustus in restoring order to the Roman world : " Also he should appear to be particularly earnest in the service of the gods ; for if men think that a ruler is religious and has a reverence

L

for the gods, they are less afraid of suffering injustice at his hands and they are less disposed to conspire against him because they believe him to have the very gods fighting on his side "[1] That religion, particularly a national religion, may be a useful prop to autocracy the history of the Reformation in England is but an example. "Augustus," said Tacitus, "seduced everyone with the sweetness of peace "; "It is a god who has made this peace for us," sang Virgil. That the world was tired of continuous civil wars in fact contributed no little to Augustus' success. These sentiments of relief and hope Augustus was naturally anxious to encourage and exploit. The theme alike of Virgil and of the *Carmen Saeculare* is thankfulness that the old bad times are gone and that a new orderly world has been inaugurated by the victory at Actium.

> "The world's great age begins anew,
> The golden years return."

Not really inconsistent with this is the policy of getting back to early Rome. Roman greatness had been built up upon Roman virtues, themselves the product of family discipline and reverence for parents, gods and established institutions.

[1] Aristotle, *Politics* 1315 a trans. Jowett.

The admirable features of simple rustic life and religion became a favourite subject of Augustan poets not merely on account of their picturesque charm but in virtue also of the moral example which they offered.

The hero of the *Aeneid* is *Pius Aeneas* and the old Roman virtues, *virtus* and *pietas*, supply the moral of the poem.   Even the Dido episode, as Warde Fowler has pointed out, reflects credit in Roman eyes upon a hero, whose behaviour has not usually found sympathy in modern sentiment. In deserting the African queen Aeneas was listening once more to the claims of right and order ; he put duty first and turned from an unauthorised passion to the responsibilities of his mission.

Though Augustus was not a religious man himself, he may well have been sincere in his belief that a healthier tone might be restored by getting back to the old religion.   He was not himself a prude in matters of sexual morality but his unsuccessful attempt to restore family morality by legislation was a complementary product of the same sincere conviction.

It is clear, too, that Augustus in getting back to the old Rome wished thereby to strengthen national feeling and national pride in the greatness of Rome. The same motive explains his attitude towards foreign religions which he sought to discourage and disparage.

This great past was further to be linked up with the yet greater future of which his new order gave promise. The empire was to be represented as being in the line of true succession from early Rome, a genuine development, not an autocracy arbitrarily imposed. That is the message of the Sixth Book of the *Aeneid*. Further the thread of continuity in this development is supplied by the Iulian family. Augustus is the lineal descendant of Aeneas, the predestined representative of Rome's greatness, and through him Augustus is personally linked with the foundation of Rome.

These or something like them were the ideas in Augustus' mind and the measures, which he took, seem designed firstly to restore an established religion and the forms of the old Roman worship, secondly to associate his person as closely as possible with this religion and to create a religious atmosphere, which would help to sanction the real autocracy which had been established under the cloak of a constitutional fiction.

In pursuance of this policy he restored the temples, whose decay Horace had regretted, and no less than eighty-two were repaired or rebuilt by him. Sacred offices, which had lapsed or become forgotten, were revived. After a gap of seventy-four years the post of *Flamen Dialis* was again filled. The *Fratres Arvales*, an ancient religious brotherhood in charge of the rites upon which the state's agricultural prosperity depended, the *Salii*, the leaping priests of Mars, and the *Luperci*, who officiated at the strange and very ancient ceremony of the *Lupercalia*, were among the most important of his restorations. These old priesthoods had lapsed with the decay of state religion, because no political power attached to the exercise of their functions. To make them attractive, Augustus gave them a social prestige. The emperor himself became a member of all the higher priestly colleges and the higher priesthoods were restricted to persons of senatorial status. Members of the imperial family held office as Arval Brethren. In the same way by emphasising the dignities he endeavoured to counterbalance the disabilities attaching to the profession of Vestal Virgins. He made the Regia, the old royal palace their place of residence, gave them the sole right of driving through the streets of Rome and in similar ways by enhancing its insignia added to the dignity of their office. He let it further be known, that had he but the good fortune to possess grand-daughters of a suitable age, he would certainly have made them Vestals.

Besides these restorations of buildings and institutions, Augustus aimed at reviving a rigid exactness in the observance of religious law. He set the example himself of a scrupulous observance of religious rules. For instance, it was inevitable that he should become *pontifex maximus ;* the holder of this office was the head of Roman religious administration and it was afterwards invariably reserved for the emperor. But important as its acquisition was to him, Augustus refused to assume it unconstitutionally, and waited until the holder, Lepidus, died in 13 B.C. In 14 B.C. when adverse omens occurred at the election of the curule aediles, Augustus immediately ordered the candidates to be withdrawn, the election to be postponed and subsequently to be carried out upon a more fortunate occasion.

So far we have been considering restorations ; in some matters Augustus introduced changes or deliberately encouraged the development of certain cults at the expense of others. In the days of the monarchy the king had been the religious head of the Roman state. Under the Republic the *pontifex maximus* had succeeded to this position

and in consequence his official residence had
always been the Regia. Augustus had become
pontifex maximus but it was practically incon-
venient for him to take up residence in the
Regia, while any association of himself with
the hated title of *rex* was the last thing which
Augustus, warned by the fate of Iulius, desired.
The solution adopted is an admirable example of
his adroitness. He covered his refusal to live in
the *Regia* by making it over to the Vestal Virgins,
thereby, as we have seen, increasing their importance and dignity, which he wished to do.
But further the law laid down the rule that the
pontifex maximus must live in a public residence.
To meet this a part of Augustus' new palace was
made over to the state. A part of the house of the
reigning emperor thus became a state residence,
an association of obvious sentimental value in
contributing to the stability of a magistracy
which was unrecognised by constitutional theory.
By a complementary stroke of policy the Vesta
of the palace was declared public. By this action
the emperor's private hearth was identified with
the hearth of the state and placed upon an equa
footing with the temple of Vesta. The effect of
these measures was in fact, that the emperor's
private house gained the associations of an official

residence and the emperor's family worship became identified with the prosperity of the state.

The cults to which Augustus gave a special prominence were those which were peculiarly associated in the popular mind with his own career or with the legendary origin of his family. A public temple of Apollo, the god to whom he owed the victory of Actium, was built upon the private property of the emperor adjoining his palace on the Palatine. Here dwelt together Apollo, Vesta and the emperor. As Ovid puts it " the one building has three gods."

> Phœbus habet partem ; Vestæ pars altera cessit.
>   Quod superest illis, tertius ipse tenet.
> State, Palatinae laurus, praetextaque quercu
>   Stet domus : aeternos tres habet una deos.[1]

Popular sentiment may not have gone quite to the lengths of poetic adulation but the association of the three in the popular mind was intimate and for Augustus' purposes useful.

Upon a yet larger scale was the building of the Augustan Forum, also upon private land belonging to the emperor (*privato solo*), which was in fact a great monument to the glorification of his family. It contained three great temples one

[1] Ovid, *Fasti*, IV, 951.

dedicated to Divus Iulius, the deified Iulius Caesar, one to Apollo of Actium and the third to Mars the Avenger. Mars had not only permitted Augustus to avenge the murder of Iulius but, by reason of his relationship to Venus from whom the Iulian clan traced their origin he was also associated with the emperor's family as well as, through Romulus, with the foundation of Rome. Since the Etruscan kings, Iupiter of the Capitol had been the great national god of Rome. Some of his importance Augustus sought now to transfer to these deities who were peculiarly associated with himself. Henceforward members of the imperial family celebrated their attainment of manhood in the temple of Mars Ultor not in that of Iupiter Optimus Maximus. The dedication of the insignia of triumph and the ceremony of the driving in of a nail to mark the conclusion of a *lustrum* were similarly transferred to the temple of Mars.

Again, upon the plea that Apollo was the source of the Sibyl's inspiration the Sibylline Books were removed from the custody of Iupiter on the Capitol and placed in that of Apollo on the Palatine.

The celebration of the *Secular Games* in June 17 B.C. is interesting in itself and usefully illustrates the ideas which inspired this policy. The idea of recurring cycles of time (*saecula*) was Greek in origin and the passage from a completed period to a new age had first been celebrated in Rome in 249 B.C. Roughly a hundred years after, in 146 B.C., the festival had been repeated to mark the passage of another *saeculum*. Although strictly speaking 17 B.C. did not fall into any cyclic relation with these previous dates, it was a part of Augustus' policy to emphasise the belief that the empire inaugurated a new era in the world's history. An oracle was therefore published which revealed that a Great Cycle of four periods of one hundred and ten years was now complete and that a new one was beginning.

The previous secular celebrations had been piacular in character. For three nights running nocturnal sacrifices to Earth and the powers below had been made at a spot called *Tarentum* in the *Campus Martius* and the ceremonies, like those of the last month of the Roman year, had been directed to the expiation of the sins of the past. Augustus gave his Secular Games a different orientation. The nocturnal sacrifices to the nether powers were retained but to them was added a daily ceremonial in which special prominence was given to Apollo, who was peculiarly associated with the new regime and to Iupiter the great god of Republican Rome. The Secular Games of Augustus looked to the future as much as to the past.

For this ceremony the poet laureate was ordered to write a hymn. Virgil had been dead for two years and the task fell to Horace whose *Carmen Saeculare* was the hymn in question. A full discussion of the contents of the song and the manner in which it was performed will be found in a paper by Warde Fowler published in his *Roman Essays and Interpretations*, p.111. As a poem it is skilful rather than inspired, a laureate's piece, dexterously composed but written strictly to order. All the deities concerned with the ritual of the three days and nights are mentioned, but Apollo and his sister, who begin the first stanza and end the last, are given a very special prominence. With them in the last stanza is linked Iupiter, and the Capitoline deities, though they are indicated only indirectly, are given a place in the middle. The deities of the nocturnal rites are invoked in the stanzas immediately following the Apolline introduction. Apollo however supplies the dominant theme of the hymn. Upon the invocations of these divine beings is strung a series of dexterous allusions to the greatness of the Roman empire, the old ideas of fertility of man and beast as dependent upon the due performance of religious duty, the increase in the birthrate to be expected from Augustus' scheme of moral reform by legislation, the connection of the imperial family through Aeneas with the foundation of Rome, the successful wars of Augustus and his restoration of the antique Roman virtues.

The song was written for a double chorus of boys and girls and it is known that it was sung both upon the Palatine and the Capitol, though whether the whole of it was repeated at both places or whether a part was sung upon one hill and a part upon the other, has been a matter of dispute. The most probable explanation is perhaps that of Warde Fowler, who points out that from both these sites the whole of Rome was visible. He supposes that the whole song was sung through on both hills and that at each singing the choruses performed evolutions turning as they sang to face the different points alluded to in the hymn.

Augustus thus associated himself with the state religion, emphasised the importance of deities especially connected with his family or his career and made his domestic hearth equivalent to the hearth of the state. His title of Augustus carried with it religious associations and the poets liken him to a terrestrial Iupiter or even, as in the verse which has been taken for the motto of Liverpool, speak of him as *deus*. But poets must not be pressed by a too literal interpretation. Lucretius had similarly spoken of Epicurus and Cicero of Plato. It will be safer to agree with Warde Fowler, that "they represent Augustus not as a deity but as having the germ of a deity in him which may be developed at his death."[1] But the idea of the possibility of the deification of a living man was in the air and the Stoic doctrine that the element of reason in man was immortal and divine provides a philosophical argument in favour of the poet's contention. It is hardly an illegitimate extension of this view to suppose it possible that in the case of a superman who is more powerful and wise than the rest of mankind the element of reason so markedly predominates that he is almost on a level with divinity.

In the eastern portions of the Mediterranean the idea of the man-god was already familiar. In the Greek world its roots were planted in the practice of worshipping important personalities as heroes immediately after their death. In the

1. A full discussion of the matter will be found in the fourth and fifth lectures of Warde Fowler, *Roman Ideas of Deity*.

period following the career of Alexander the Great, who himself laid claim to a more than mortal origin and status, the deification of powerful human beings had become common in the Hellenistic East. When Euhemerus developed his doctrine of the origin of gods, he was in fact arguing backwards from the analogy of the royal Saviours (*Soteres*) and Benefactors (*Euergetai*) of his age.

The political conditions which had promoted the growth of this practice in the Eastern Mediterranean had been in some respects not dissimilar to those in Italy during the last century of the Republic. Old institutions had broken down, times were bad and uncertain; the gods appeared of little real help in trouble. The real arbiters of the fate of individuals appeared to be blind Chance (*Tyche*) or great and powerful kings. The worship of Chance, whom the Romans identified with the old Italian deity Fortuna, had widely spread in the Roman world and though the idea of deifying an individual dead man or of worshipping a living emperor were neither of them native to Italy, the conditions were favourable to their introduction. With the ideas current in the East Romans were of course familiar and provincial governors had upon occasion been the recipients of semi-divine honours.

Had he wished to do so, it is improbable that Augustus could have prevented the worship of the living emperor in the East. In fact the worship of Augustus and Roma, which was the worship of the emperor, rather than of the individual man who happened to be sitting on the throne, coupled with the greatness of the Roman Empire, spread throughout the provinces and became a bond which united the whole Roman dominions. Students of the early history of Christianity will remember that the refusal of Christians to conform with its official ritual was in no small measure the cause of their being branded as disloyal to the Roman state.

For the deification of emperors after their death, a practice which became the rule, Augustus provided the model when he recognised the apotheosis of the great Dictator and dedicated the temple to Divus Iulius, but in Italy he refused to permit the direct worship of his living self. A compromise however presented itself which gratified popular desire and at the same time connected what was almost the worship of Augustus with the old religion of the family and of the farm.

It will be remembered that the Genius of the master of the house had from very early times been an especial object of family ritual. This

provided an analogy of unimpeachable respect-
ability and native origin for the worship of the
Genius of the emperor by his subjects.

Again a part of the old ritual of the farm had
consisted in the worship of Lares Compitales at
the intersection of the boundaries of properties.
This rustic cult has been adapted to the town
where the Lares were worshipped at the cross-
roads. The urban cult was popular in character
and was controlled by collegia whose members
were drawn from the lower orders. These, with
other democratic associations, had been suppressed
owing to the unscrupulous use made of such
clubs for political purposes. Augustus now
reorganised Rome into fourteen regions, each
of which was subdivided into *vici*. He revived
the *collegia compitum* and at the junctions of the
boundaries of these subdivisions were erected
shrines containing three images. Two represented
the Lares ; the third associated with them was
the Genius of Augustus. The third partner in
this triad naturally predominated in popular
estimation and the three became known as Lares
Augusti.

From Rome the worship of the Lares Augusti
spread all over Italy. It gave rise to the order of
augustales membership of which provided a safe

outlet for the social ambition of wealthy freedmen who were debarred by their status from holding municipal office.

There is no doubt that in the achievement of his immediate political aim of creating a religious atmosphere to give support and sanction to the imperial system, Augustus was successful, but a revival of the old Roman religion in any real sense was impracticable. There was in fact no possibility of breathing life into bones so dry. Augustus, could restore ancient liturgies and priesthoods but he could not recreate the old conditions of life and society which had given them birth. For good or evil the process, which is commonly called progress, is inexorable ; there is no return and the clock cannot be put back. The old Roman religion and the old family virtues, which Augustus also sought to recapture, were as impossibly remote as the virtuous and happy peasantry of whom Tiberius Gracchus had dreamed. The institution of the empire in itself made a revival of a city state religion impossible. For the empire put an end to free political life and this both in Greece and Rome was the very life blood of city state religion.

If it was impossible for a cosmopolitan empire to recapture the social and political environment

M

of early Roman religion, it was no less impossible to recover the intellectual environment of its worshippers. Philosophy could not be unlearned nor could the Romans, even if they had so wished, return to the unlettered and simple morality of their ancestors and forget the iconoclastic speculation, which they had learned from Greece. Further individualism had come to its own and could not now be dethroned. But for individualism there was no satisfaction in the old civic and corporate worship. The demand of the individual soul for religious self expression, the anxieties about the prospect of a future life or the growing sense of the need of salvation could not be stifled. Indeed, the sense of this personal religious need was made more acute by the loss of political liberty, which diverted the mental activities of men into channels other than those of politics, and by the increasing influence of women, to whom the ancient forms of worship had little to offer. Hence the rapidity with which the Eastern cults spread from the lower classes of the cosmopolitan city into the upper strata of society. The variety, similarities and rivalry of these Oriental religions however belong more properly to the history of the Empire and lie beyond the scope of these lectures.

INDEX

179